HISTORY MAP BOOKS

BRITISH SOCIAL AND ECONOMIC HISTORY 1760–1980

This book is ... turned on ...

Philip Sauvain

Basil Blackwell

Teacher's Notes

This book has been designed to give examination students a clear and concise outline structure of the essential elements of the social and economic history of Britain since 1760. Inevitably some topics have had to be omitted, in order that the significant developments of the last two hundred years can stand out in sufficient detail to emphasise their role in shaping modern society.

The maps, graphs, diagrams and charts, which together form the backbone of this book, have been planned as simply as possible to ensure that the relevant facts are presented in an easily assimilated form. In particular the maps have been envisaged as a type of shorthand, or mnemonic, of particular value for students working towards an external examination.

This book may be used in various ways; by some as an introduction to the subject; by others as a study framework to be amplified with the use of other teaching materials. It may also be of service as a revision summary. Above all it is a history map book designed to support, consolidate and clarify work undertaken from the textbook.

© Philip Sauvain 1985
First published 1985

Basil Blackwell Limited
108 Cowley Road
Oxford
OX4 1JF

ISBN 0 631 91480 3

Printed in Great Britain by Bell and Bain Ltd., Glasgow

ACKNOWLEDGEMENTS

The author and publisher wish to thank the following for permission to reproduce photographs:
BBC Hulton Picture Library 36; Mansell Collection 48; Trades Union Congress Library 52.

Contents

The Open Field System: Britain in 1760

In 1700 a large part of England was still farmed in medieval open fields. These huge fields, a hundred hectares or more in size, were each divided into a large number of long strips. A well-to-do farmer might hold a lot of these strips, some on good farmland and others on poorer ground. By 1700 many medieval strips had been acquired by the luckier or more prudent farmers and combined to make fields enclosed by hedges or fences; but most farmers still had their land divided among the two or three open fields of the village. The poorest farmers scraped a living from a few isolated strips; and some, the cottagers, had none – although they did have the right to graze their cattle and sheep on the common land.

The open fields were used for growing crops. They were unfenced, and straying animals could wander across them. One open field was usually sown with wheat, the second with barley or peas, and the third left *fallow* (without crops). Cattle and sheep grazed on the stubble and weeds in the fallow field and their manure helped to fertilise the soil and make it fresh for a new crop of corn the following year.

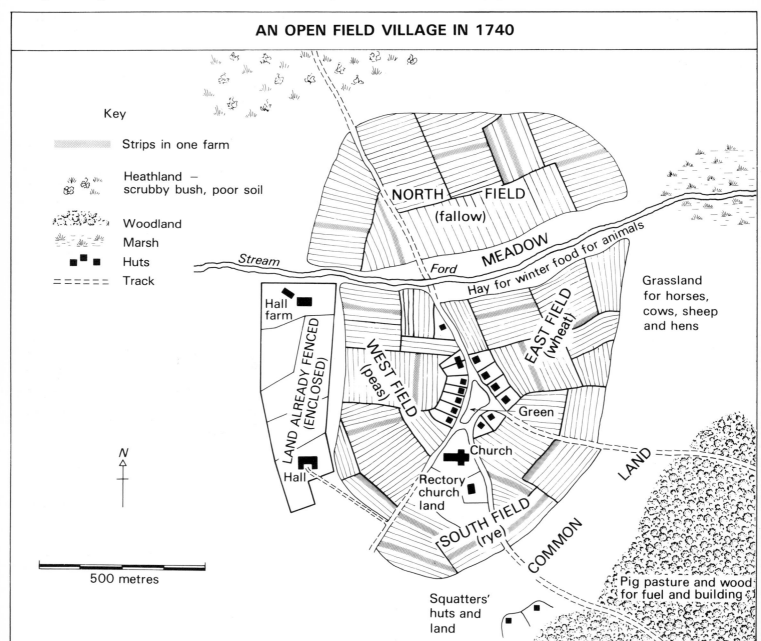

AN OPEN FIELD VILLAGE IN 1740

Key

Strips in one farm

Heathland – scrubby bush, poor soil

Woodland

Marsh

Huts

Track

NORTH FIELD (fallow)

Stream   Ford   MEADOW

Hay for winter food for animals

Hall farm

LAND ALREADY FENCED (ENCLOSED)

WEST FIELD (peas)

EAST FIELD (wheat)

Grassland for horses, cows, sheep and hens

Green

Church

Hall

Rectory church land

SOUTH FIELD (rye)

COMMON LAND

N

500 metres

Squatters' huts and land

Pig pasture and wood for fuel and building

THE OPEN FIELD SYSTEM

ADVANTAGES

1 People grow their own food. They don't have to rely on other people for their basic needs. They are self-employed and free to work for as long or as short a time as they please.

2 Most villagers have some land. Even the landless can graze their animals on the common land.

3 Because the strips are scattered throughout the open fields most people live in cottages in the centre of the village. They help their neighbours when the fields are ploughed and sown. Few farmers own enough horses or oxen to pull a plough; so they share out the tasks—each farmer contributing one of the beasts for the plough team.

4 The villagers have other rights as well as grazing; such as the right to get timber, turf and bracken from the wastelands and woodland near the village.

5 Having a number of different strips in each open field means that most people have a fair share of the best and worst land.

6 Village tradesmen and craftsmen like the blacksmith, carpenter and wheelwright supply almost every need.

DISADVANTAGES

1 The strips are too small to make it worth using implements like a seed drill. Corn is usually sown by hand—a very wasteful and inefficient method.

2 Farmers waste time travelling from one distant strip to another.

3 The weeds from strips belonging to poor or lazy farmers quickly spread to the next-door land.

4 Because cattle and sheep graze with all the other animals on the common land, they are unable to breed from the better quality animals. The cattle are thin. Milk yields are low. Pests and diseases spread quickly, since it is impossible to separate healthy animals from the others.

5 Crop yields are often poor because the soil needs manure and other fertilizers. Many open fields are badly drained but it is difficult for individual farmers to drain their isolated strips of land.

6 Having a fallow year every three years means that crops can only be grown on two-thirds of the arable land in any one year.

7 Too many animals graze on the common pasture lands. Few fodder crops (e.g. turnips) are grown; so only a few animals can be kept during the winter.

WHY MORE FOOD WAS NEEDED, 1700–1820

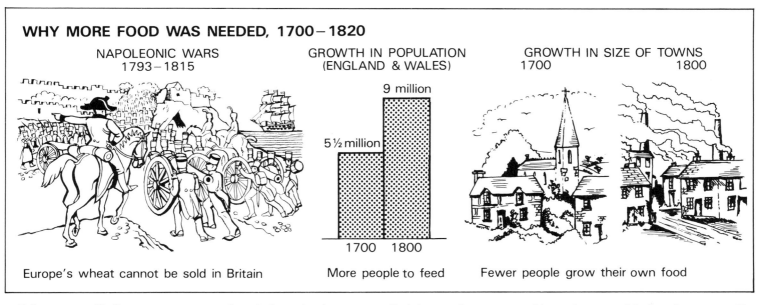

NAPOLEONIC WARS 1793–1815 — Europe's wheat cannot be sold in Britain

GROWTH IN POPULATION (ENGLAND & WALES) — 9 million, 5½ million, 1700 1800 — More people to feed

GROWTH IN SIZE OF TOWNS 1700 1800 — Fewer people grow their own food

Most small farmers grew food for their own families rather than crops to sell for cash. But during the eighteenth and nineteenth centuries there was an increasing demand for food, so it paid farmers to increase production. Many farmers tried new methods of farming (see pages 8–9) but this was only feasible where the open fields had been enclosed (see pages 6–7). Enclosure meant putting the strips of land together into compact fields and surrounding them with hedges, walls or fences.

??????????????????????????????

1 Look at the map and then write a detailed description of an open field village.

2 What were the weaknesses of the open field system of farming? What were its main advantages?

Enclosures

If you compare the map on this page with the one on page 4 you can see what happened to the countryside when the open fields were enclosed. Hedges, fences, walls and ditches enclosed small fields, so that the countryside looked like a patchwork quilt from the air.

Enclosure made the larger landowners richer, since they could afford to try out new machines, crops and farming methods. British farms more than doubled the food they grew between 1700 and 1850. But this destroyed the old way of life in the countryside. The high cost of enclosure meant that some poor farmers had to sell their plots to the large landowners. The countryside changed from one where most people owned some land to one where most farm workers had none.

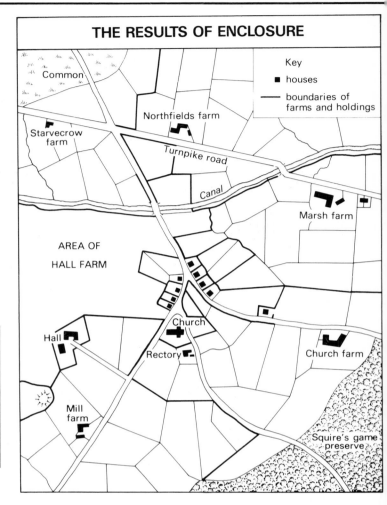

THE RESULTS OF ENCLOSURE

Key
■ houses
— boundaries of farms and holdings

Common

Northfields farm

Starvecrow farm

Turnpike road

Canal

Marsh farm

AREA OF HALL FARM

Church

Hall

Rectory

Church farm

Mill farm

Squire's game preserve

?????????????????????????????

1 Imagine you are a farmer holding a number of strips in the open fields of your village. Write a summary of the conversation you have had with two other farmers – one arguing for enclosure and the other against.

2 Why did enclosure favour the richer farmers, even though the commissioners often did their best to share the land fairly?

ENCLOSURES

ADVANTAGES

1 Compact farms instead of scattered strips. Farmers save time.

2 Farmers are able to drain their fields, use fertilisers, kill weeds by hoeing, and employ other new farming methods.

2 Farmers are able to breed from the best animals to yield more milk, better meat and finer wool.

4 Farmers hold more land than they did before since the meadows, commons and waste land are also shared out.

5 The value of farmland rises and food production increases.

DISADVANTAGES

1 Many poorer people are deprived of their rights to cut timber, turf, or bracken and to graze their animals on the commons.

2 Everyone has to pay the costs of the survey. Many small farmers have to sell their land to the richer farmers. Some get jobs as farm workers, some go to the towns seeking work, others continue to live in the village in desperate poverty.

3 Rents increase because there is a demand for land, but labourers' wages fall because many people are in need of jobs.

4 The old way of life changes. Farmers no longer live in the villages. Many village occupations disappear, such as the *hayward* who looked after the meadows and the *pinder* who rounded up stray cattle. Farmers buy machines from factories rather than tools made by village craftsmen such as the smith and carpenter.

HOW ENCLOSURE WAS CARRIED OUT

1

The richer farmers get together and agree to take action to try to get the open fields of the village enclosed.

2

Because they hold over 80% of the land in the village they are able to get a special *Enclosure Act* passed by Parliament.

3

Commissioners are paid (by the villagers) to come and survey the open fields and commons in the village. They draw maps showing the land everyone holds.

4

They hear the claims of poor people who say they have a right to graze animals on the commons.

5

The Commissioners award the land to those people who held strips in the old open fields. Some farmers get better land than others. The common land is also enclosed, although some is left for the poorer people. Some of the poorest villagers are left without any land at all. Some are evicted from their cottages.

6

Hedges are planted.

7

Ditches are dug.

8

Roads are built.

9

Farmhouses are erected among the fields of the new farms.

10

Some poorer farmers have to sell their plots to pay the costs of enclosing the land.

New Farming

Farmers gradually changed their farming methods in the eighteenth and nineteenth centuries. But there was no sudden revolution in farming. Changes which began in the seventeenth century took two hundred years or more to come to fruition. Even though Jethro Tull invented the seed drill in 1701, many farmers still sowed their corn by hand until at least 1820.

??????????????????????????????

What new methods were used by British farmers in the eighteenth and early nineteenth centuries? How did they help them to grow bigger and better crops and bigger and better animals?

SEVEN REASONS WHY NORFOLK FARMERS ARE SUCCESSFUL

1 By enclosing.
2 By the use of marl and clay.
3 By the introduction of an excellent course of crops (Turnips—Barley—Clover or Ryegrass—Wheat).
4 By the culture of turnips, well hand-hoed.
5 By landlords granting long leases.
6 By the culture of clover and ryegrass.
7 By the country being divided chiefly into large farms.

ARTHUR YOUNG 1771

THE 'IMPROVING' FARMERS

ROBERT BAKEWELL (1725–1795) bred sheep (Leicesters and New Leicesters) and Longhorn cattle at Dishley, in Leicestershire. By selective breeding, he trebled the weight put on by a typical fat sheep but the mutton was fatty and not of the best quality. He was highly regarded by the farmers of his day but some criticised his methods.

VISCOUNT 'TURNIP' TOWNSHEND (1674–1738) used the Norfolk rotation, improved the land on his estate at Raynham in Norfolk with *marl* (a clay with lime in it), and popularised the use of root crops. (But he didn't introduce them into Britain.)

JETHRO TULL (1674–1741) was an eccentric Berkshire farmer who was opposed to the use of animal manures. Instead he advocated horse-hoeing to kill weeds. To make this easier to accomplish he invented the seed drill in 1701, which sowed corn in rows.

THOMAS COKE (1752–1842) used many of the new ideas on his large estate at Holkham in Norfolk—such as long leases, crop rotations, land drainage, plantations and selective breeding of sheep and cattle. But the benefits these improvements could make to a farm had long been known. His success was in persuading many other farmers to adopt the new ideas. In this way, like 'Turnip' Townshend, he was as important to the new farming as the inventors.

ARTHUR YOUNG (1741–1820) had been unsuccessful as a farmer but this didn't stop him advising others. He toured Britain, wrote many reports on farming, and showed how enclosure and the new farming methods had brought an increase in food production and profit to the farmers who had adopted them. In 1793 he became the first secretary of the newly-founded Board of Agriculture. He helped to spread new ideas to farmers who might otherwise have ignored them.

This four Wheel Drill Plow, with a Seed and a Manure Hopper, was first Invented in the Year 1745 and is now in Use with Wm Ellis at Little Gaddesden near Hempstead in Hertfordshire, where any person may View the same. It is so light that a Man may Draw it but Generally drawn by a pony or little Horse.

An eighteenth-century seed drill.

HOW A FARMER IMPROVED THE LAND

FERTILISERS

Marl, lime, clay, seaweed, night soil (human manure) from the towns, waste products from industry and animal dung improve the fertility of the soil and make heavy soils easier to cultivate. Factories begin making artificial fertilisers in the 1840s.

NEW CROPS

Root crops, such as turnips, help to 'clean' the fields, since it is easy to weed between the rows with a hoe.

Grasses, such as clover, lucerne and ryegrass are grown as part of the crop system to make hay.

These new crops take their nourishment from different layers in the soil. Their leaves rot down to add plant foods to the soil. They are used as fodder for the animals in winter; so more horses, cattle, sheep, pigs and poultry can be kept.

BREEDING

A number of farmers, such as Robert Bakewell and Thomas Coke experiment with selective breeding. The offspring of cows yielding above-average quantities of milk can be mated to produce a new generation of high-yielding cows.
By the early nineteenth century some prize bulls, rams and other top quality breeding animals fetch very high prices (over £1000 in some cases).

CROP ROTATIONS

These help farmers to increase their output, instead of leaving one field fallow in every three.

LONG LEASES

By agreeing to *lease* (rent) farms to tenants for long periods, big landowners like Thomas Coke encourage their tenant farmers to improve their land.

NEW MACHINES

Jethro Tull's seed drill sows corn seed in rows; his horse-hoe is used to kill weeds. The Rotherham plough (1760) can be pulled by two or four horses instead of by a team of three or six. An all-iron plough is made in Ipswich in 1808 and a steam plough in Devonshire in 1832. Mechanical reapers (1826), and threshing machines worked by horses turning a wheel, or by a steam engine (1786), are among many other inventions.

DRAINAGE

New methods of draining waterlogged fields are used to make them suitable for crops or pasture. Draining ploughs dig ditches and these are filled with rubble and covered with soil. Water drains into these channels.

PLANTATIONS

Some farmers plant trees to provide timber for commercial uses (such as pit props), and also to shelter their farms from the wind.

The Corn Laws

During the Napoleonic Wars with France (1793–1815) Britain could not buy grain from Europe because the French controlled most of the Continent. As a result, the price of British wheat rose steeply, and farmers made fat profits. At the end of the war, foreign wheat could be imported again. The farmers feared that this would be sold more cheaply than British wheat, so they would be forced to bring down their high prices. Most MPs were landowners, and they persuaded the Government to take action to protect the farmer.

TIME LINE

1815 The Corn Laws 'prohibit the import of wheat until the price rises to 80/- (£4) per quarter'. There are similar limits on the purchase of foreign rye, peas, beans, barley and oats. As a result the cost of bread is higher than it would be if cheap foreign wheat were allowed into Britain. The Corn Laws bring profits to farmers and landowners but at the expense of poor people, whose main food is bread.

1839 The Anti Corn Law League is founded by Richard Cobden and John Bright to persuade the Government to repeal the Corn Laws. They want Free Trade between countries, so that foreign wheat can be bought as easily as British wheat. In return British manufacturers will be able to sell more of their goods abroad, since foreign governments will be encouraged to lower the duties (taxes) they put on British manufactures. Lower bread prices will mean less poverty.

1846 The Tory prime minister, Sir Robert Peel, convinced that the Corn Laws are an obstacle to British trade with the rest of the world, repeals the Corn Laws. The decision is greeted with horror and landowners say it will bring ruin to British farmers.

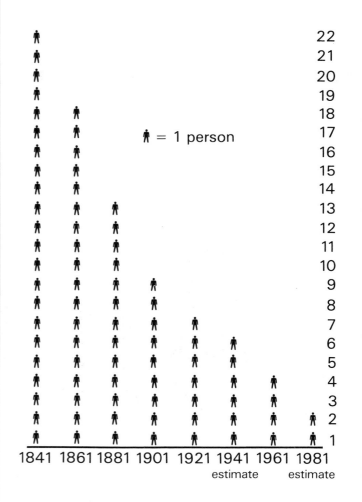

PERCENTAGE OF WORKING PEOPLE EMPLOYED IN FARMING 1841–1981

= 1 person

1841 1861 1881 1901 1921 1941 1961 1981
estimate estimate

(In 1801 36 people in every 100 were engaged in farming in Great Britain).

The Golden Age of Farming

Despite the gloomy forecasts of Britain's farmers and politicians, the price of wheat remained more or less the same after the repeal of the Corn Laws in 1846. One reason for this was that the population of Britain was growing so rapidly there were always more mouths to feed. Although more corn came into the country it was not enough to pull down the price of British wheat – yet. No foreign wheat-grower had large surpluses of wheat to spare for export. The rich prairie areas of Canada and the United States had hardly been developed at this time. They did not really threaten British wheat farmers until railways were built across North America.

In fact this was a 'golden age' of prosperity for farmers and landowners. Their farms were becoming more efficient, so it cost them less to grow crops and rear livestock. Yet the prices they got for their produce were much the same. New methods of farming were slowly being introduced. (Some of these improvements can be seen in the diagram.) Large numbers of farm labourers were still employed but from about 1860 onwards farming gradually became less and less important as the main source of employment for workers in Britain. New machines sometimes meant that fewer workers were needed on the farms. At the same time the factories and towns took a bigger share of the population each year.

??????????????????????????????

1. Explain what the Corn Laws were and why they were eventually repealed.
2. What was the 'Golden Age of Farming'?

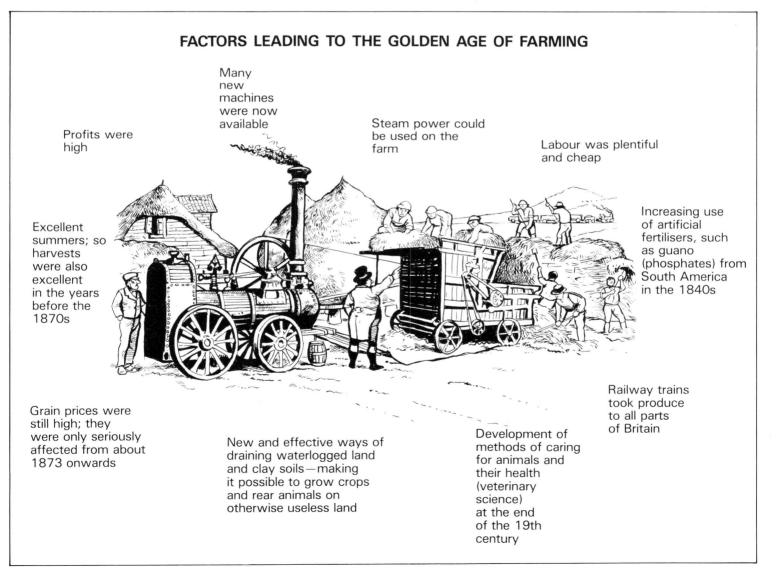

FACTORS LEADING TO THE GOLDEN AGE OF FARMING

Profits were high

Many new machines were now available

Steam power could be used on the farm

Labour was plentiful and cheap

Excellent summers; so harvests were also excellent in the years before the 1870s

Increasing use of artificial fertilisers, such as guano (phosphates) from South America in the 1840s

Grain prices were still high; they were only seriously affected from about 1873 onwards

New and effective ways of draining waterlogged land and clay soils—making it possible to grow crops and rear animals on otherwise useless land

Development of methods of caring for animals and their health (veterinary science) at the end of the 19th century

Railway trains took produce to all parts of Britain

Depression in Farming

The Golden Age of Farming was succeeded, in about 1873, by a period of over 40 years when British farming was in the doldrums. Many farmers went out of business

---

THE DEPRESSION IN FARMING

Causes

1 Wet weather caused a succession of bad harvests which reduced the amount of corn produced by Britain's farmers. The wheat was also attacked by mildew.

2 The price of wheat fell sharply because American wheat began to reach Britain in large quantities. Railways across Canada and the USA brought cheap wheat from the prairies to the Atlantic ports.

3 From 1882 onwards, refrigerated ships made it possible to ship meat from New Zealand and Argentina.

4 Farmers complained about paying new taxes such as the rate for education after 1870. The Education Act of 1870 also deprived them of cheap child labour in the fields.

5 Diseases such as foot and mouth disease (cattle) and sheep rot added to their problems.

Effects

1 The area of land under the plough decreased as more and more arable farmers changed to livestock farming. By concentrating on dairy cows they hoped to beat off foreign competition, since milk had to be sold fresh. Milk could now come by rail from Devon to London.

2 Some farmers went into market gardening, producing vegetables for the rapidly growing populations of industrial towns and cities. Others turned to poultry or fruit.

3 Cheap foreign corn helped British livestock farmers, since maize and other foodstuffs could be used as cheap fodder.

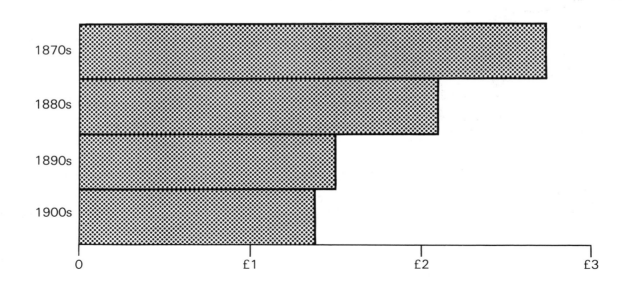

PRICE OF WHEAT PER QUARTER

Farming in the 20th Century

During the First World War imports of foreign wheat, meat and other foods were curtailed by German submarine attacks on merchant ships in the Atlantic. The Government paid subsidies to farmers in 1917 to encourage them to grow more wheat and oats.

But after the war the subsidies were removed and British farming suffered, particularly in the Depression years of the early 1930s. Eventually the Government reintroduced the subsidies and restricted foreign imports. Shortages of food during and after the Second World War gave farmers a further boost. Guaranteed prices, farm subsidies and other incentives have helped farmers ever since. When the UK and the Irish Republic joined the European Community in 1973 farmers benefited from the Common Agricultural Policy of the EEC. This is designed to keep up farm prices, and lessen the effects of foreign competition.

Since 1945 there has been a dramatic increase in output from British farms – accomplished at a time when the number of workers employed in agriculture has fallen rapidly (by 35% between 1951 and 1971).

????????????????????????????

1 Imagine you are an old farmer in 1880. Describe the changes you have seen since 1809, when you first started work on a farm at nine years old.
2 What were the most significant changes in British farming between 1870 and 1970? Why did they occur?

FARMING IN THE TWENTIETH CENTURY

Chemical sprays and pesticides to kill insects and prevent diseases

Combine harvesters since 1928

Many other new machines, such as potato-picking machines, manure spreaders, forage harvesters

Mains water and electricity on most farms

New and better-yielding varieties of corn seed and other crops

Artificial fertilisers

New methods of preventing and curing diseases in animals

Government and Common Market payments help to guarantee good prices for farm produce

Factory farming methods to make animals and poultry produce more food more rapidly

Powerful tractors (fewer people needed to work on the farm)

The Domestic System

Before 1760 there were very few factories in Britain. Industries were small and organised by individual merchants. Instead of wool being spun, woven and finished by a large number of workpeople in one factory, the different jobs were done in different places. This was called the domestic system, because most people worked in their own homes, Spinning and weaving were sometimes a way of adding to the income earned from cultivating a small plot of land. Domestic woollen workers worked long hours, from dawn to well after dark. Young children were put to work by their parents. Working in the factories did not necessarily mean a harder life for textile workers. Sometimes it did; but sometimes they were better paid and better fed than when they worked for themselves.

??????????????????????????

1 What were the chief characteristics of the domestic system?
2 What were its main advantages and disadvantages?

DANIEL DEFOE DESCRIBES THE YORKSHIRE WOOLLEN INDUSTRY AROUND 1720

'First, the wool itself, taken from the sheep's back . . .

. . . is sold to the clothier (wool merchant).'

'Every clothier must keep one horse at least to fetch home his wool and his provisions from the market, to carry his yarn to the spinners . . .

. . . his manufactures to the fulling mill and when finished to the market to be sold.'

'Among the clothiers' houses are scattered a great number of cottages, in which the workmen, women and children are employed from the youngest to the oldest; scarce anything above four years old, but its hands were sufficient for its own support.'

'We saw houses full of lusty fellows, some at the dye-vat . . .

some at the loom . . .

others dressing the cloths.'

'The women and children carding . . .

. . . or spinning.'

THE TEXTILE INDUSTRY IN THE EARLY EIGHTEENTH CENTURY

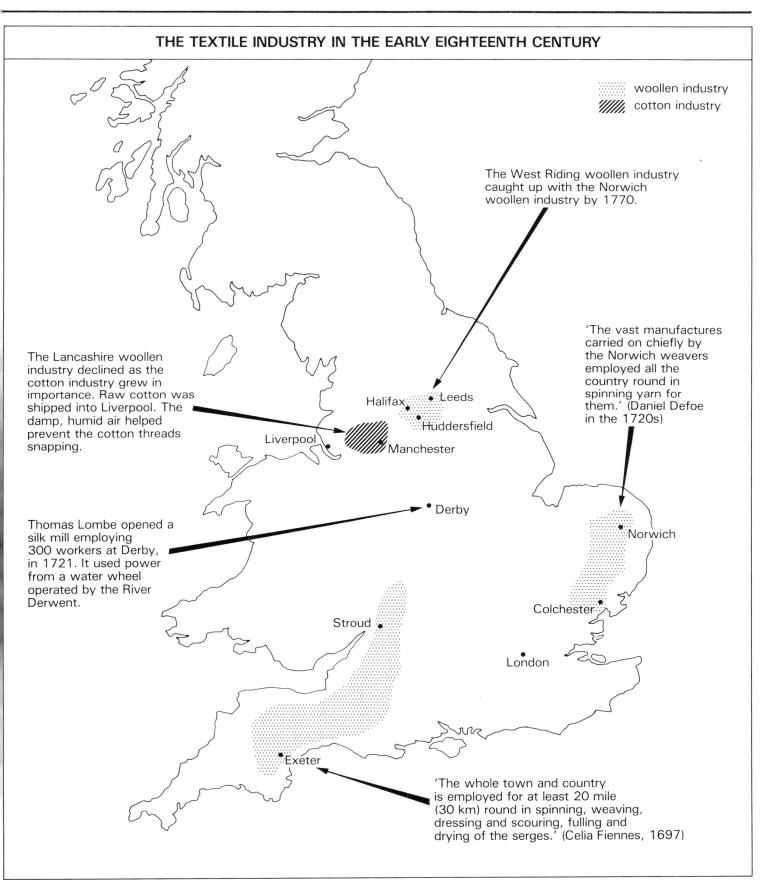

woollen industry
cotton industry

The West Riding woollen industry caught up with the Norwich woollen industry by 1770.

'The vast manufactures carried on chiefly by the Norwich weavers employed all the country round in spinning yarn for them.' (Daniel Defoe in the 1720s)

The Lancashire woollen industry declined as the cotton industry grew in importance. Raw cotton was shipped into Liverpool. The damp, humid air helped prevent the cotton threads snapping.

Thomas Lombe opened a silk mill employing 300 workers at Derby, in 1721. It used power from a water wheel operated by the River Derwent.

'The whole town and country is employed for at least 20 mile (30 km) round in spinning, weaving, dressing and scouring, fulling and drying of the serges.' (Celia Fiennes, 1697)

Halifax · Leeds
· Huddersfield
Liverpool · Manchester
Derby
Norwich
Colchester
Stroud
London
Exeter

The Industrial Revolution: Textiles

The change from the domestic system to the factory system came when new machines were invented which could only be used in special buildings where water power or steam power was available. The first machine to have a real effect was Kay's *flying shuttle*. This could more than double the amount of cloth a single weaver could produce in a day. But the handloom weavers were opposed to it, fearing that many jobs would go if it was widely used. A similar reaction from cotton spinners met the *spinning jenny* and the *water frame* when they were first introduced.

The *water frame* was powered by a water wheel. Richard Arkwright built the world's first cotton spinning mill in 1771 on the banks of the River Derwent at Cromford in Derbyshire. He chose Derbyshire because he wanted his factory to be situated away from Lancashire where cotton

IMPORTANT INVENTIONS IN THE TEXTILE INDUSTRY IN THE EIGHTEENTH CENTURY

INVENTION	The FLYING SHUTTLE 1733	The SPINNING JENNY 1767	The WATER FRAME 1769
INVENTOR	JOHN KAY, of Bury, Lancashire.	JAMES HARGREAVES of Blackburn, Lancashire.	RICHARD ARKWRIGHT of Preston, Lancashire.
PURPOSE OF INVENTION	To enable one weaver to do the work of two.	To enable spinners to produce more yarn to meet the demand created by the flying shuttle.	To enable the spinning process to be mechanised, using power from a water wheel.
PREVIOUS METHOD	By hand. The weaver threaded a shuttle carrying the weft thread through the long warp threads on the loom. With broadloom cloth two weavers were needed, one on each side.	By hand and foot. Using a spinning wheel in which straightened cotton or woollen fibres were spun (twisted) and wound on to a spindle.	By hand (spinning wheel or spinning jenny) in the home.
NEW METHOD	The weaver pulled a cord which sent the shuttle *flying* through the warp threads.	The *jenny* (named after his wife) could spin yarn on eight spindles at once.	Using power from a water wheel to spin cotton on to four spindles on each frame.
ADVANTAGES	Only one weaver was needed to weave broadloom cloth; the flying shuttle speeded up the weaving process. The workforce could double its output of cloth.	Could be used at home—it didn't require a factory or mill building. Produced eight times as much yarn as the spinning wheel.	Produced a strong and tough yarn. The machines could go on indefinitely, powered by water.
DISADVANTAGES	Fewer workers were needed to make the same amount of cloth; so some weavers regarded the shuttle as a threat to their jobs.	Produced a fine but weak yarn which broke easily. Like the flying shuttle it was feared by spinners who thought their livelihood was in danger.	The yarn wasn't as fine as that produced by the spinning jenny. The frame could only be housed in a factory, since it needed water power.

workers had already destroyed other spinning machines, such as those of Kay at Bury and Hargreaves at Blackburn.

Woollen manufacturers were much slower than those in the cotton industry to adapt the new machines for use in their mills. There were still only 5000 power looms in the woollen mills as late as 1838 – over 50 years after Cartwright's invention of 1785. Most weavers were still handloom weavers. But by 1878 there were 146 000 power looms in use.

???????????????????????????
Imagine you are an old textile worker in 1800. Write a description of the changes you have seen in the cotton industry since you first began work in 1730.

INVENTION	The SPINNING MULE 1779	The POWER LOOM 1785	The COTTON GIN 1793
INVENTOR	SAMUEL CROMPTON of Bolton, Lancashire.	EDMUND CARTWRIGHT, a Leicestershire clergyman.	ELI WHITNEY, an American inventor.
PURPOSE OF INVENTION	To combine the merits of the spinning jenny with those of the water frame.	To use steam engines to power looms and speed up the weaving process.	To extract cotton fibre from the cotton bolls and separate it from the seeds.
PREVIOUS METHOD	The spinning jenny or the water frame.	The handloom with or without the flying shuttle.	By hand.
NEW METHOD	The *spinning mule*, so-called because it was a cross between the spinning jenny and the water frame.	Enabled the loom to be operated by steam engines.	Tugged the cotton fibre away from the boll, leaving the seeds behind.
ADVANTAGES	Spun cotton on to 48 spindles at the same time. The yarn was finer than the water frame could produce yet stronger than that from the spinning jenny.	Greatly speeded up the weaving process. Helped manufacturers to produce cloth of the same quality.	Enabled a single worker to extract 25 kg of cotton fibre a day, instead of 0.5 kg by hand. Encouraged cotton growers to produce more.
DISADVANTAGES	Needed water power or steam power and a factory building.	Had to be used in a factory. It destroyed the way of life of thousands of handloom weavers.	Encouraged the slave trade in the southern states of the United States.

The Industrial Revolution: Coal Mining

Coal has been mined in Britain since the Middle Ages. The early miners found coal lying close to the surface; it was only when this had been used up that miners really began to have problems. These became more acute during the eighteenth century, when the demand for coal rose rapidly. It was used (as coke) to smelt iron ore; and to heat the boilers which produced the steam needed to power steam engines. From about 1800 coal gas was used for street and domestic lighting, and with the expansion of the railways and the introduction of steamships in the nineteenth century, the demand for coal continued to grow.

?????????????????????????????

1 Which inventions in the coal-mining industry made it possible for the colliery owners to sink even deeper shafts to get at the coal?
2 Write an account of the way in which the coal-mining industry developed between 1700 and 1850.

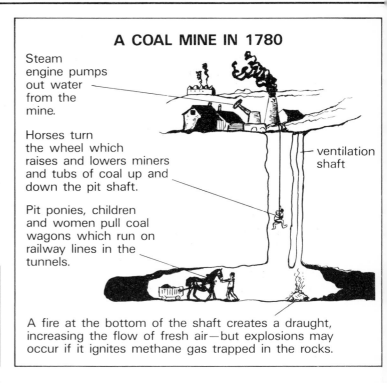

A COAL MINE IN 1780

Steam engine pumps out water from the mine.

Horses turn the wheel which raises and lowers miners and tubs of coal up and down the pit shaft.

Pit ponies, children and women pull coal wagons which run on railway lines in the tunnels.

ventilation shaft

A fire at the bottom of the shaft creates a draught, increasing the flow of fresh air—but explosions may occur if it ignites methane gas trapped in the rocks.

MAIN COAL-MINING AREAS IN GREAT BRITAIN

Main coal-mining areas

Fife
Lothian
Lanarkshire
Ayrshire
Northumberland and Durham
Cumberland
Lancashire
Yorkshire
Derbyshire
Nottinghamshire
North Wales
North Staffs
Warwickshire
Shropshire
Leicestershire
South Wales
Forest of Dean
Bristol
Kent
Somerset

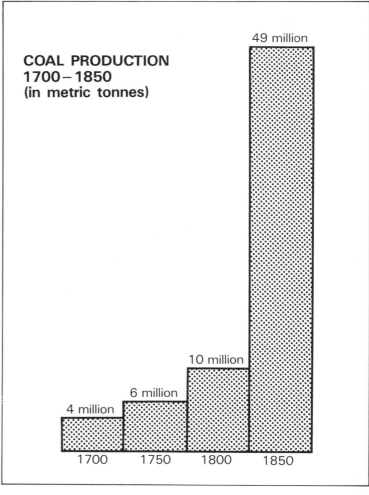

COAL PRODUCTION 1700–1850 (in metric tonnes)

49 million
10 million
6 million
4 million

1700   1750   1800   1850

DEVELOPMENTS IN COAL MINING 1700–1850

OLD METHODS	NEW METHODS
Cutting coal	
Semi-naked miners loosened the coal with picks and then shovelled it into baskets or tubs.	Miners continued to use picks well into the twentieth century, despite the invention of coal-cutting machines in the 1860s.
Transport underground	
At first the baskets of coal were carried by women and children to the pithead. Railway lines were later laid along the underground passageways and small boys and crouching women, with ropes or chains round their waists, hauled the tubs of coal to the bottom of the pit shaft.	In the early nineteenth century, steam engines began to power the pit winding gear which lifted coal to the surface. Underground steam engines were used to wind cables attached to the coal wagons.
Working conditions	
Small girls, boys of four or five and women were employed underground as well as men. Lord Shaftesbury said that near Oldham (Lancashire) 'the ways are so low that only little boys can work in them'.	Lord Shaftesbury played a big part in persuading Parliament to pass the Coal Mines Act of 1842 which prohibited the employment of girls, women and boys under ten, working underground.
Roof collapse	
Miners left pillars of coal to support the roof but this was unreliable and many were buried alive when a roof collapsed.	In the later 'longwall' method of mining the miners cut all the coal at the coal face but used pit props of timber, or iron, to support the roof.
Flooding	
Coal mines were said to be *'so wet that the people have to work all day over their shoes in water, at the same time that the water is constantly dripping from the roof'.*	In 1712 Thomas Newcomen invented a steam engine to pump water out of a coal mine near Birmingham. His pump was later improved by James Watt.
Lighting	
Lighting underground was extremely poor, since the naked flame from a candle could easily cause an explosion by setting fire to methane gas (fire-damp) released when coal was mined.	Sir Humphry Davy invented the safety lamp in 1815. The flame inside was protected by a screen made of fine wire gauze which prevented the methane gas from being ignited.
Ventilation	
From about 1660 onwards miners lit fires below the up-shaft so that it acted like a chimney, expelling foul air from the underground workings, and drawing in fresh air down the down-shaft.	In about 1807 John Buddle used a steam powered air pump at a Tyneside colliery. Mechanical fans powered by steam engines were used in the 1830s, although some collieries continued to use furnaces for many years.

The Industrial Revolution: Iron and

Until the end of the seventeenth century the British iron industry relied on charcoal to smelt iron ore. So iron works were usually situated in forest areas, near deposits of ironstone. They were also built near water, so that water wheels could be used to power the bellows and operate the huge hammers that forged the iron into shape. By the turn of the century the iron industry was facing a crisis. Much of the timber in the forests had been used up as fuel, or taken to build houses and ships. Then, in 1709, Abraham Darby I devised a new method of smelting iron ore, using coke instead of charcoal. This meant that iron works no longer relied on timber; in the future they were built near coal.

With the old method, only a small amount of iron ore could be heaped on top of the charcoal. Too much would prevent the blast of air from the bellows raising the temperature high enough to melt the iron in the ore. With Darby's method, much larger furnaces could be built, since the coke could support a heavier weight of iron ore. The new coke-fired blast furnaces were also able to raise the iron to much higher temperatures, so

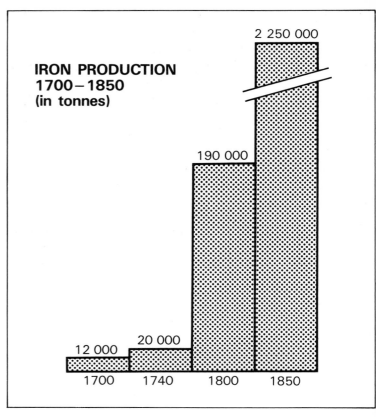

IRON PRODUCTION 1700–1850 (in tonnes)

Year	Production
1700	12 000
1740	20 000
1800	190 000
1850	2 250 000

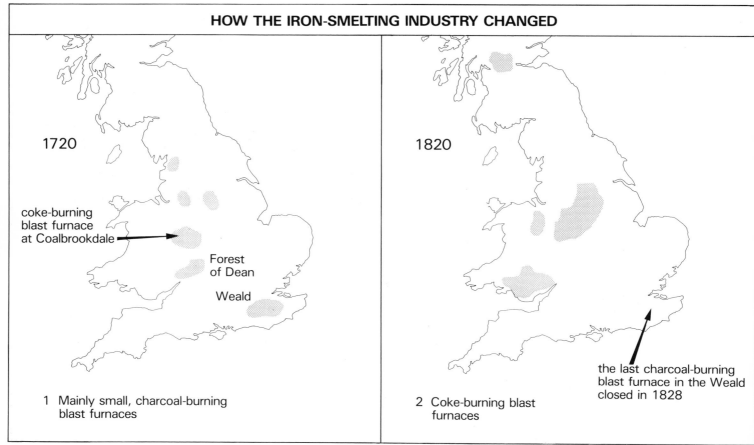

HOW THE IRON-SMELTING INDUSTRY CHANGED

1720

coke-burning blast furnace at Coalbrookdale

Forest of Dean

Weald

1 Mainly small, charcoal-burning blast furnaces

1820

the last charcoal-burning blast furnace in the Weald closed in 1828

2 Coke-burning blast furnaces

Steel

that it could be run off as liquid iron into moulds, called *pigs* (hence the term pig iron).

Abraham Darby's son and grandson continued his work at Coalbrookdale. Other important developments came from Benjamin Huntsman, John Wilkinson and Henry Cort. Steam power also helped, since steam engines could take the place of the water wheel. In its turn the iron and steel industry provided the materials and equipment (such as accurately-bored cylinders) needed to manufacture steam engines and machinery for other industries, such as textiles.

?????????????????????????

1 Look at the maps on these pages and at the map of the coalfields on page 18. Describe and explain the reasons for the changes in the British iron and steel industry between 1700 and 1830. How did the innovations of the eighteenth century affect the siting of new ironworks in Britain?
2 In what ways did the development of the iron and steel industry affect other industries in Britain at that time?

DEVELOPMENTS IN THE IRON AND STEEL INDUSTRY IN THE EIGHTEENTH CENTURY

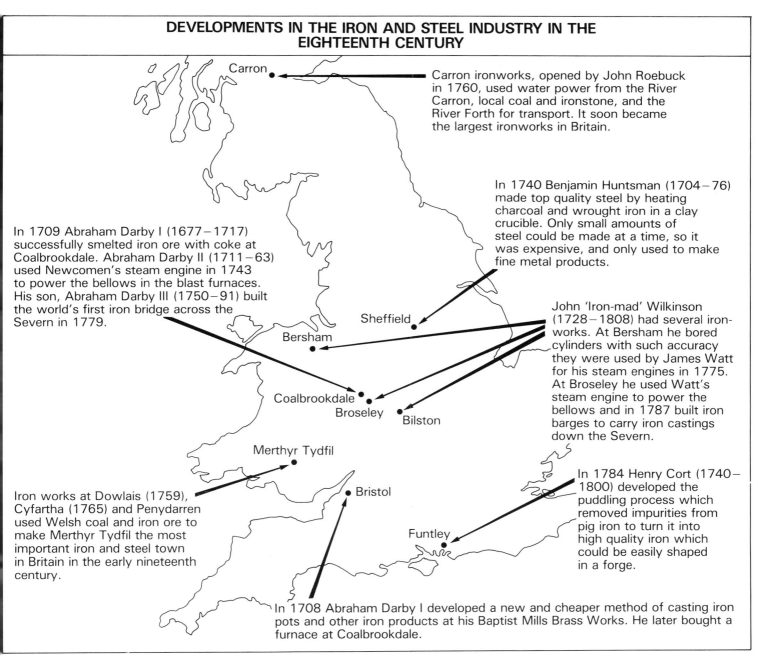

Carron ironworks, opened by John Roebuck in 1760, used water power from the River Carron, local coal and ironstone, and the River Forth for transport. It soon became the largest ironworks in Britain.

In 1740 Benjamin Huntsman (1704–76) made top quality steel by heating charcoal and wrought iron in a clay crucible. Only small amounts of steel could be made at a time, so it was expensive, and only used to make fine metal products.

In 1709 Abraham Darby I (1677–1717) successfully smelted iron ore with coke at Coalbrookdale. Abraham Darby II (1711–63) used Newcomen's steam engine in 1743 to power the bellows in the blast furnaces. His son, Abraham Darby III (1750–91) built the world's first iron bridge across the Severn in 1779.

John 'Iron-mad' Wilkinson (1728–1808) had several iron-works. At Bersham he bored cylinders with such accuracy they were used by James Watt for his steam engines in 1775. At Broseley he used Watt's steam engine to power the bellows and in 1787 built iron barges to carry iron castings down the Severn.

In 1784 Henry Cort (1740–1800) developed the puddling process which removed impurities from pig iron to turn it into high quality iron which could be easily shaped in a forge.

Iron works at Dowlais (1759), Cyfartha (1765) and Penydarren used Welsh coal and iron ore to make Merthyr Tydfil the most important iron and steel town in Britain in the early nineteenth century.

In 1708 Abraham Darby I developed a new and cheaper method of casting iron pots and other iron products at his Baptist Mills Brass Works. He later bought a furnace at Coalbrookdale.

The Industrial Revolution: Steam Power

The invention of the steam engine in the eighteenth century turned Britain from an agricultural country into the world's first industrial nation.

The first steam pump was invented by Thomas Savery in 1698 but it was superseded by Thomas Newcomen's steam engine in 1712. This was known as an atmospheric engine because it used air pressure (atmospheric pressure) to push the piston down. Newcomen's engine was used to pump water out of mines. Its main disadvantages were that it was too large and cumbersome for the amount of power it produced; it wasn't easy to convert its see-saw, up-and-down motion into rotary motion (i.e. like that of a waterwheel); and it was uneconomical, since it wasted most of the heat from the boiler by alternately heating and cooling the cylinder.

In 1769, James Watt, a Scottish engineer, improved upon Newcomen's engine by designing and finally making a steam engine with a separate condenser. The cylinder always remained hot, so the engine produced more power yet used much less coal than the equivalent Newcomen engine. At first it was difficult to build a reliable engine, since considerable precision was needed in the manufacture of its valves and cylinders. But in 1774 Watt teamed up with Matthew Boulton at the Soho Works in Birmingham and there they made the world's first true steam engine. In this machine it was steam that pushed the piston down *not* air pressure.

The Boulton-Watt steam engines were highly successful. In 1782 Watt made further improvements to the engine to make it double-acting, so that steam drove the piston up as well as down, and he converted the up and down motion of the beam into rotary action by using a device known as the sun and planet system. It was this rotary steam engine which was later used to power the machinery in Lancashire's rapidly expanding cotton mills.

Later engineers made the steam engine many times more efficient and developed engines to power railway locomotives, steamships, traction engines and many other different types of machinery.

?????????????????????????????

1 What were the main types of power in use in 1700?
2 How and why were new forms of mechanical power developed in the eighteenth century?

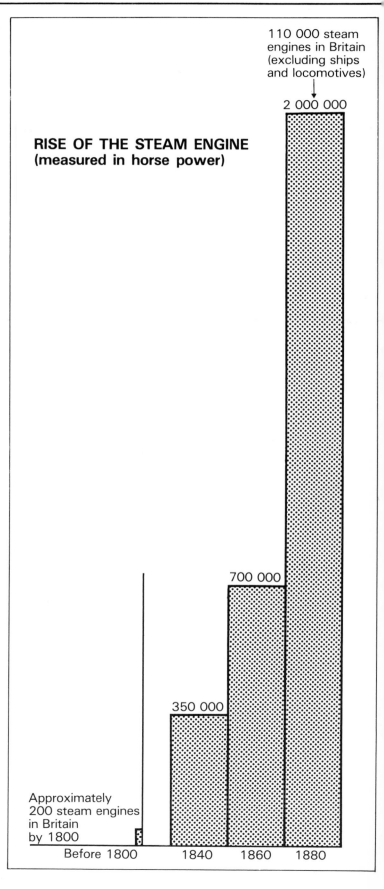

RISE OF THE STEAM ENGINE
(measured in horse power)

110 000 steam engines in Britain (excluding ships and locomotives)

2 000 000

700 000

350 000

Approximately 200 steam engines in Britain by 1800

| Before 1800 | 1840 | 1860 | 1880 |

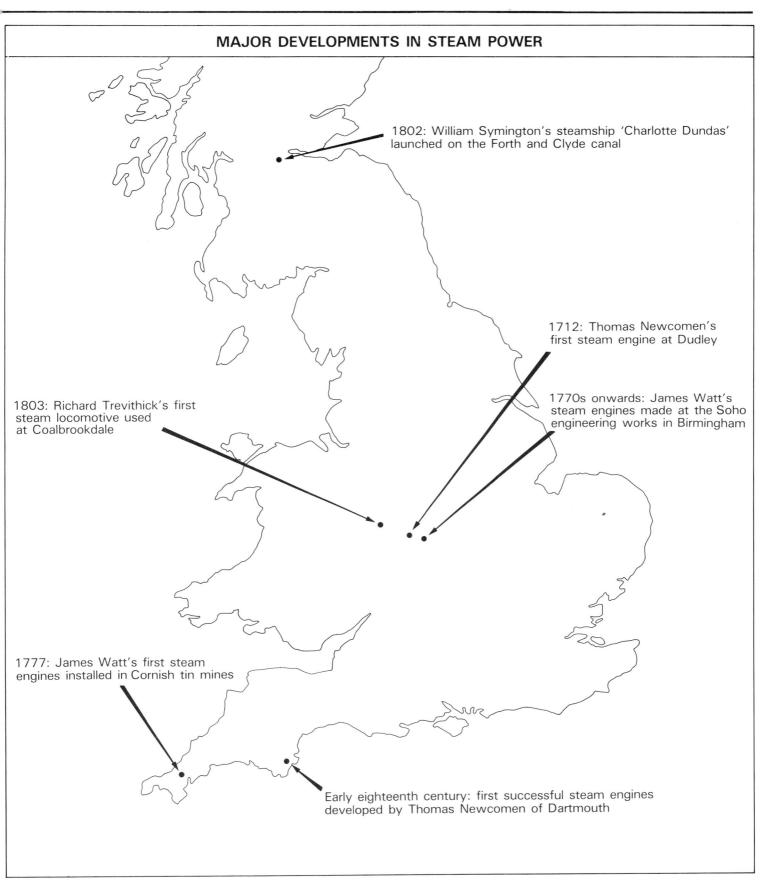

MAJOR DEVELOPMENTS IN STEAM POWER

1802: William Symington's steamship 'Charlotte Dundas' launched on the Forth and Clyde canal

1712: Thomas Newcomen's first steam engine at Dudley

1770s onwards: James Watt's steam engines made at the Soho engineering works in Birmingham

1803: Richard Trevithick's first steam locomotive used at Coalbrookdale

1777: James Watt's first steam engines installed in Cornish tin mines

Early eighteenth century: first successful steam engines developed by Thomas Newcomen of Dartmouth

The Factory Acts

The swift and uncontrolled growth of industry at the end of the eighteenth century, and in the early years of the nineteenth century, often led to appalling and dangerous working conditions in mines and factories. These came to light in government reports and through the investigations of philanthropists like Lord Shaftesbury. They urged Parliament to bring in laws to protect working people. Slowly they made progress.

TIME LINE

1819 FACTORY ACT applied only to cotton workers. It prohibited the employment of children under 9 and restricted daily working hours to 12 for children under 16. Not effective since it wasn't easily enforced.

1833 FACTORY ACT prohibited the employment of children under 9 in all textile works and restricted daily working hours to 9 (children under 13) and 12 (ages 13 to 18). More effective, since government inspectors were appointed to see it was enforced. Their reports drew attention to other evils as well.

1842 COAL MINES ACT prohibited the employment underground of girls, women and boys under 10.

1844 FACTORY ACT restricted daily working hours to 12 (weekdays) and 9 (Saturdays) for women in textile factories and to 6½ hours for children under 13. Manufacturers had to screen dangerous machinery to prevent accidents.

1847 TEN HOURS ACT restricted daily working hours to 10 for women and young people aged 13 to 18. Not as effective as had been hoped.

1850 TEN HOURS ACT modified to 10½ hours per day (plus 1½ hours for meals). Workers had Saturday afternoons off as well as Sundays.

1867 FACTORIES AND WORKSHOPS ACT made these provisions apply to all works employing five or more workers.

??????????????????????????????

1 Imagine you are a television producer in 1832 and wish to expose the appalling factory conditions in many parts of Britain. Describe the things you would include in your programme.
2 What changes were made in factory working conditions between 1800 and 1850?

THE COTTON MILL

Unguarded machines — accidents are common

Extremely noisy — deafening to the ear

Nauseating smells — permanent reek of oil and grease

Damp, humid and hot — workers sometimes stripped to the waist

Cruelty by overseers — children often flogged

Long working hours — over 12 hours a day

Very young children employed

Spread of diseases among factory workers — 'factory fever'

Cotton dust choking eyes and lungs

WORKING CONDITIONS IN THE EARLY NINETEENTH CENTURY

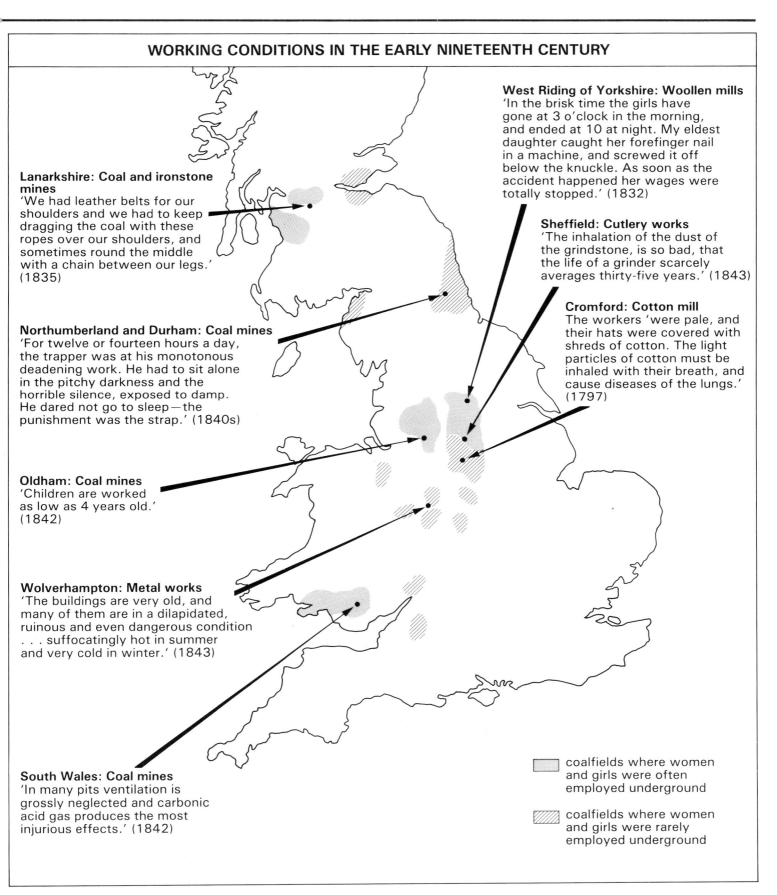

West Riding of Yorkshire: Woollen mills
'In the brisk time the girls have gone at 3 o'clock in the morning, and ended at 10 at night. My eldest daughter caught her forefinger nail in a machine, and screwed it off below the knuckle. As soon as the accident happened her wages were totally stopped.' (1832)

Lanarkshire: Coal and ironstone mines
'We had leather belts for our shoulders and we had to keep dragging the coal with these ropes over our shoulders, and sometimes round the middle with a chain between our legs.' (1835)

Sheffield: Cutlery works
'The inhalation of the dust of the grindstone, is so bad, that the life of a grinder scarcely averages thirty-five years.' (1843)

Cromford: Cotton mill
The workers 'were pale, and their hats were covered with shreds of cotton. The light particles of cotton must be inhaled with their breath, and cause diseases of the lungs.' (1797)

Northumberland and Durham: Coal mines
'For twelve or fourteen hours a day, the trapper was at his monotonous deadening work. He had to sit alone in the pitchy darkness and the horrible silence, exposed to damp. He dared not go to sleep—the punishment was the strap.' (1840s)

Oldham: Coal mines
'Children are worked as low as 4 years old.' (1842)

Wolverhampton: Metal works
'The buildings are very old, and many of them are in a dilapidated, ruinous and even dangerous condition . . . suffocatingly hot in summer and very cold in winter.' (1843)

South Wales: Coal mines
'In many pits ventilation is grossly neglected and carbonic acid gas produces the most injurious effects.' (1842)

coalfields where women and girls were often employed underground

coalfields where women and girls were rarely employed underground

Workshop of the World

By 1850 Great Britain stood head and shoulders above the other industrial nations. Twice as many people worked in mining and manufacturing industries as in agriculture. In every other country in the world more, usually many more, people worked on farms than in factories. Britain's closest rival in Europe was Germany, but it wasn't until the 1950s that she too had twice as many workers in industry as in agriculture.

For much of the nineteenth century Britain was the 'workshop of the world', producing over three-quarters of the world's ships and between a third and a half of the world's coal, iron and cotton yarn. Britain's main rivals could not match her output of steel until the 1890s (USA in 1890 and Germany in 1893), and it was the twentieth century before they caught up in coal production (USA in 1900 and Germany in 1920).

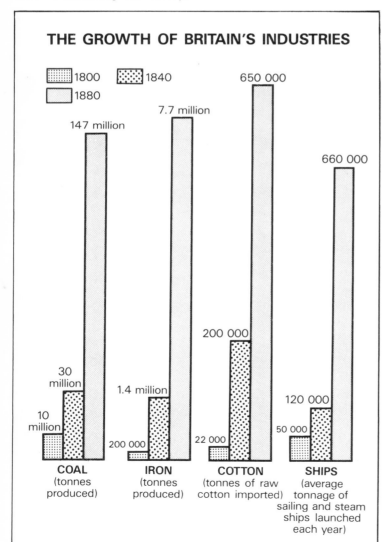

THE GROWTH OF BRITAIN'S INDUSTRIES

1800   1840   1880

COAL (tonnes produced): 10 million, 30 million, 147 million

IRON (tonnes produced): 200 000, 1.4 million, 7.7 million

COTTON (tonnes of raw cotton imported): 22 000, 200 000, 650 000

SHIPS (average tonnage of sailing and steam ships launched each year): 50 000, 120 000, 660 000

WHY BRITAIN BECAME THE 'WORKSHOP OF THE WORLD'

1 She had a **reliable and stable government.** No wars were fought on British soil in the nineteenth century. Manufacturers could invest money in new factories and machines knowing they would reap the benefits. Europe, by contrast, was torn by civil wars, rebellions and wars between countries. Germany was divided into many small states and not united until 1871. The USA was still exploring the frontier lands of the west and was ripped apart by the Civil War between North and South (1861–65).

2 She had a **large Empire** which provided many of the raw materials she needed (e.g. wool) and which took many of her manufactures in return.

3 She had **many clever inventors and enterprising manufacturers,** such as Abraham Darby, Thomas Newcomen, James Watt, Richard Arkwright, Josiah Wedgwood, Edmund Cartwright and Henry Bessemer, whose inventions and new methods gave Britain a commanding lead over other countries between 1700 and 1860. The development of the steam engine in Britain, and the ease with which British coal could be mined then, gave her industries an enormous advantage over those in other countries which still relied on handicrafts and water power.

4 She had the **raw materials** necessary for the rapid growth of the iron and steel industry. Coal and iron ore were often found close to each other.

5 She had a **large and cheap workforce;** and her population grew rapidly in the nineteenth century.

6 She had a **large and expanding market at home** for her manufactures.

7 She was the **first country to develop an extensive network of canals and later railway lines** (see pages 38–41), which made it easy and cheap for manufacturers to get raw materials to their factories, and send manufactured goods to their customers or to the ports for export overseas.

8 She owned more ships than the rest of the world put together, pioneered **ironclads** (ships with hulls encased in metal) and steamships, and controlled much of the world's trade.

??????????????????????????????

1 Why did Britain become the 'workshop of the world'?
2 What does the graph tell you about the growth of these four industries in the nineteenth century?

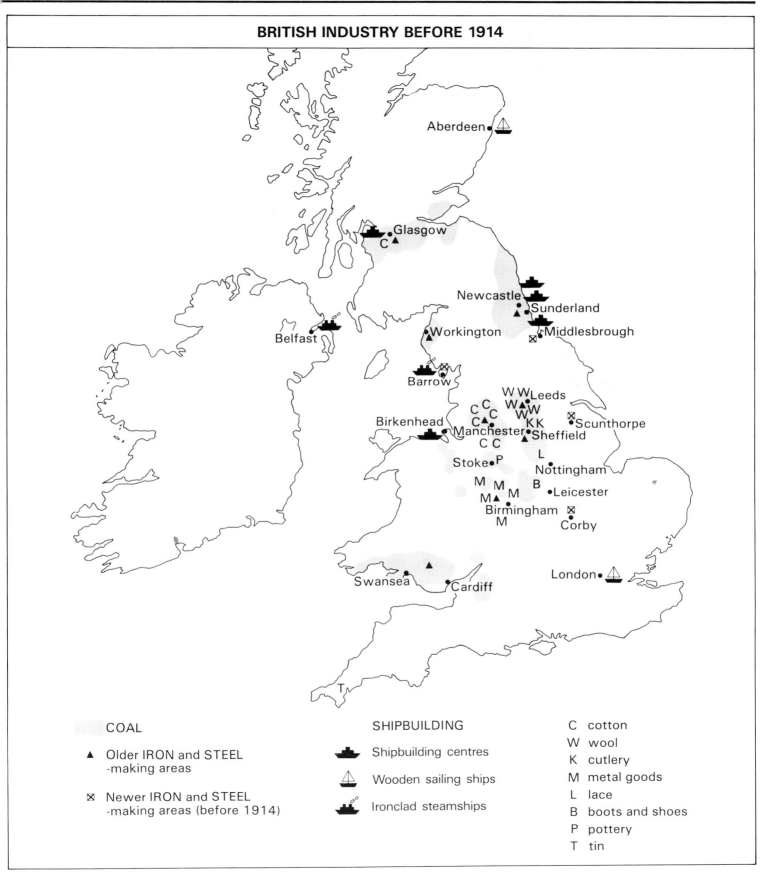

BRITISH INDUSTRY BEFORE 1914

Aberdeen

Glasgow
C

Newcastle
Sunderland
Workington
Middlesbrough

Belfast

Barrow

Birkenhead
W W Leeds
W
C C C W W
C C KK
Manchester Sheffield
C C
Scunthorpe

Stoke P
L
Nottingham

M M B
M M M Leicester
Birmingham
M Corby

Swansea
Cardiff
London

T

COAL

▲ Older IRON and STEEL
-making areas

⊠ Newer IRON and STEEL
-making areas (before 1914)

SHIPBUILDING

Shipbuilding centres

Wooden sailing ships

Ironclad steamships

C cotton
W wool
K cutlery
M metal goods
L lace
B boots and shoes
P pottery
T tin

The Growth of the Steel Industry

In the first half of the nineteenth century steel was an expensive metal to produce, costing about £75 a tonne. In 1856, however, Henry Bessemer invented a revolutionary new process which was so efficient that it cut the cost of making steel to less than £20 a tonne. His converter could produce

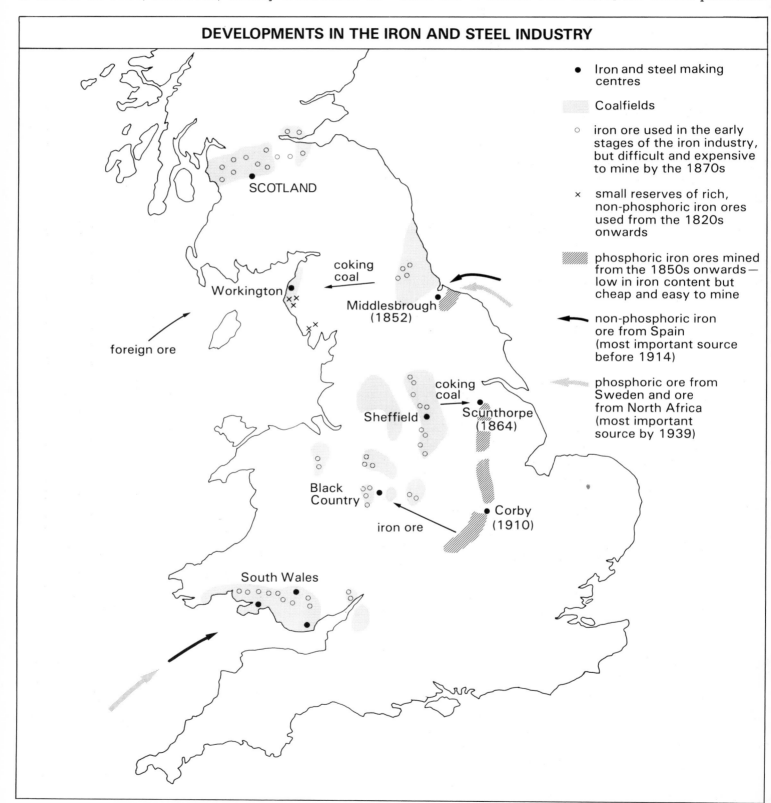

DEVELOPMENTS IN THE IRON AND STEEL INDUSTRY

- ● Iron and steel making centres
- Coalfields
- ○ iron ore used in the early stages of the iron industry, but difficult and expensive to mine by the 1870s
- × small reserves of rich, non-phosphoric iron ores used from the 1820s onwards
- phosphoric iron ores mined from the 1850s onwards— low in iron content but cheap and easy to mine
- ◄ non-phosphoric iron ore from Spain (most important source before 1914)
- ◄ phosphoric ore from Sweden and ore from North Africa (most important source by 1939)

SCOTLAND

coking coal

Workington

Middlesbrough (1852)

foreign ore

coking coal

Sheffield

Scunthorpe (1864)

Black Country

iron ore

Corby (1910)

South Wales

twenty times as much steel as the old puddling furnace, in less than a quarter of the time.

Unfortunately, Bessemer's 'acid' steel method could only be used with iron from non-phosphoric ores. These were only found in Cumbria, so nine new steel works were built there in the 1870s, near Workington and Barrow-in-Furness. Following this an open-hearth method of making 'acid' steel was developed. This was easier to control than Bessemer's process, and just as cheap, although it took a lot longer.

The open-hearth furnace also required non-phosphoric ores, so Britain began to import these from northern Spain. Previously, very little foreign ore had been used. By now, however, the easily-won ore in the British coalfields had been exhausted and it was becoming increasingly difficult to obtain iron ore. Competition from foreign ores threatened the older iron and steel works in the South Wales mining valleys. Gradually these were replaced by new steel works on the coast.

Large new reserves of phosphoric ore had already been discovered in central and eastern England. This was cheap and easy to mine, but low in iron content. In 1877 the Gilchrist-Thomas process of making 'basic' steel was invented. Unlike the 'acid' steel method, this could use phosphoric ores.

Middlesbrough was particularly well placed to take advantage of the new developments: it was situated on the coast (where it was easy to obtain imports of foreign ore) and lay between Cleveland iron ore to the south and Durham coking coal to the north. Middlesbrough grew from a village of 200 in 1800 to a large industrial town with about 100 000 people by 1900. Scunthorpe and Corby were also new steel towns, which grew rapidly in the twentieth century.

Unfortunately for Britain, the new process also helped the steel industry in Europe, where much of the iron ore was phosphoric. In 1883 Germany made one million tonnes of steel (half that produced by the UK). By the 1890s she was producing the same amount as the UK, and in 1913 she made eighteen million tonnes (twice that made in the UK). The United States drew ahead in the 1890s, too. The British steel industry also suffered badly during the Depression years of the 1930s. There was less foreign demand for steel, partly because many other countries had built up strong iron and steel industries of their own.

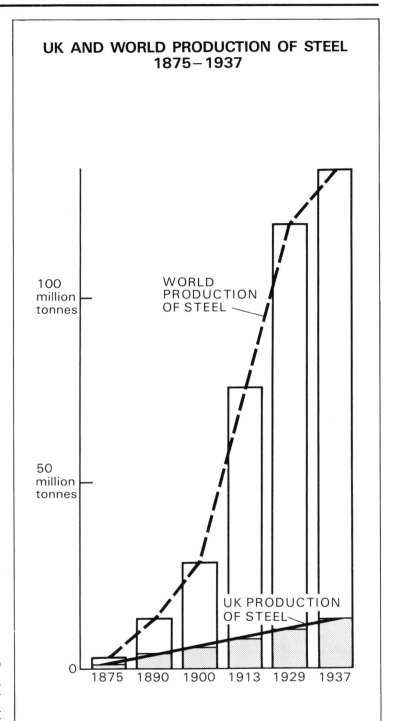

UK AND WORLD PRODUCTION OF STEEL 1875–1937

100 million tonnes

WORLD PRODUCTION OF STEEL

50 million tonnes

UK PRODUCTION OF STEEL

0   1875   1890   1900   1913   1929   1937

???????????????????????????

1 Describe the changes in the British iron and steel industry after 1856. What effect did these changes have on the location of the industry?

2 Look at the map and classify the different iron and steel making areas according to their situation with regard to supplies of coal and iron ore.

British Industry in the 20th Century

Most of the great inventions and discoveries of the eighteenth century were made by British inventors. This helped Britain to become the world's first industrial nation. But by 1900 the other big powers were catching up fast. German inventors built the first motor car and Americans the first aircraft. The Americans also developed a large motor industry using mass-production methods, while Germany took the lead in the manufacture of chemicals and the production of electricity.

Many of these newer industries did not use steam powered machinery or need large supplies of coal. Advantages which had helped Britain to become the 'workshop of the world' were of little value in the twentieth century. Although many industries grew, they didn't keep pace with those in foreign countries; so Britain's share of world markets fell. Coal, steel, cotton and shipbuilding all suffered badly from foreign competition and the effects of the Depression of the 1930s (see pages 60–61). Industries which did well in the 1920s and 1930s were those which made consumer goods for the home market, such as cars, electrical goods (radios, vacuum cleaners) and processed foods.

WHY NEW INDUSTRIES WERE LOCATED IN SOUTH-EASTERN ENGLAND

1 Manufacturers aimed their products mainly at the home market, so they built their factories in or close to London with its huge population and excellent road and rail communications.

2 They used electricity (*or* oil *or* gas) for power, so there was no need to seek a site on a coalfield.

3 The raw materials they used could be transported by lorry easily and cheaply, so there was no need to seek a site close to a quarry, port or iron and steel works.

4 London and the south-east was considered cleaner and more attractive than the depressed and smoke-ridden industrial towns of the north.

REASONS FOR THE DECLINE OF SOME BRITISH INDUSTRIES IN THE TWENTIETH CENTURY

COAL	Reached the peak of production in 1913 with over 290 million tonnes. Fell to half that output by 1970.	**1** Increasing use of oil (heating, industry, ships, cars, trains), electricity and natural gas (instead of coal gas). **2** Decline in foreign demand for British coal because it was too expensive (much of the easily-mined coal had been exhausted). Many collieries were too small and owners couldn't afford to modernise them (e.g. by using coal-cutting machines). **3** Competition from countries like Germany, Poland and the USA helped to halve British coal exports in the inter-war period. Foreign countries wanted less coal because of the Depression.
COTTON	Reached the peak number of spindles in 1920 with nearly 60 million. Fell to half that number by 1950.	**1** Increasing use of synthetic fabrics (such as rayon, nylon and terylene) especially after World War Two. **2** Foreign competition. Countries like Japan and India were able to produce cotton goods more cheaply. Japan's cotton industry had overtaken Britain's by 1935. **3** Many Lancashire cotton mills had out-dated machinery.
SHIPBUILDING	Reached peak output in 1920 (about 2 million tonnes of shipping) dropping to under 200 000 tonnes in 1933 and rising to 1 million tonnes just before World War Two.	**1** Foreign competition—countries like Japan, Poland and Greece were able to build ships more efficiently for less money, partly because wages were often lower there than in the UK. **2** British shipyards were slow to use new methods of building ships. **3** The Depression in the 1930s meant there was less foreign trade, so *fewer* merchant ships were needed *not more*. Over 60% of Britain's shipyard workers were unemployed in 1932 and 1933. **4** The shipbuilding industry expanded during the First World War. When peace came production dropped (once the shipyards had replaced the ships sunk during the war).

BRITAIN'S SHARE OF WORLD PRODUCTION

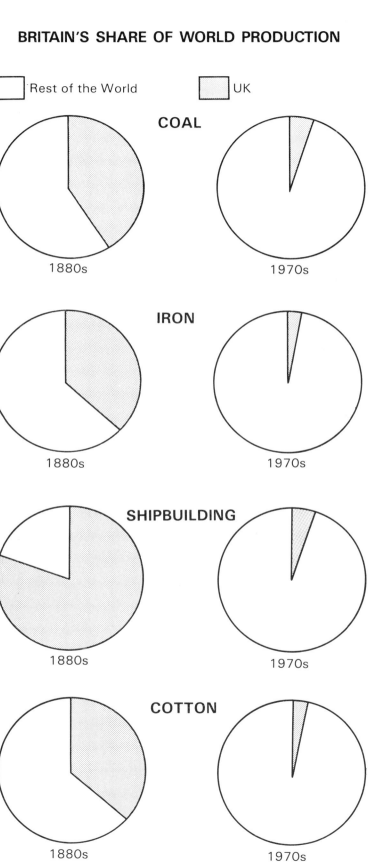

□ Rest of the World   ▨ UK

COAL
1880s   1970s

IRON
1880s   1970s

SHIPBUILDING
1880s   1970s

COTTON
1880s   1970s

JOBS IN BRITISH INDUSTRY

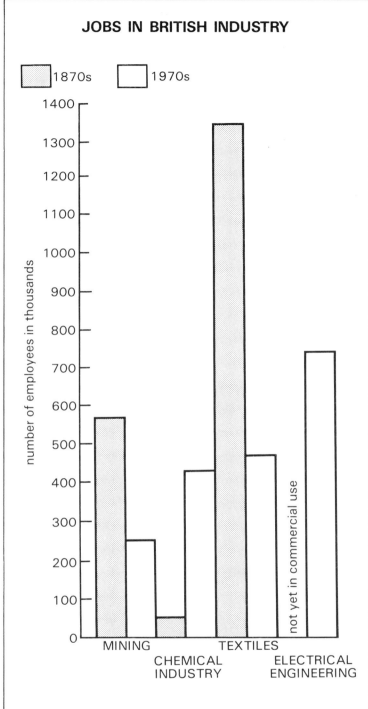

▨ 1870s   □ 1970s

number of employees in thousands

1400
1300
1200
1100
1000
900
800
700
600
500
400
300
200
100
0

MINING   TEXTILES
   CHEMICAL   ELECTRICAL
   INDUSTRY   ENGINEERING

not yet in commercial use

??????????????????????????????

1 By what date was Britain no longer the 'workshop of the world'?
2 Look at the graphs. Explain the differences you can see between the figures for the 1870s and 1880s and those for the 1970s.

New Industries

The motor industry

In 1913, Henry Ford introduced moving assembly lines at his car factory in Detroit, America. This was the start of mass-production methods which were to revolutionise the motor industry all over the world. The assembly lines carried partly-finished vehicles past long lines of workers, who each added to, or altered, the body or engine in front of them. Ford was so successful that by 1923 his works were producing nearly two million vehicles – twice as many as the rest of the world put together!

Before 1914 most British cars were made by hand, and could cost as much as a house to buy. Ford's mass-production ideas were soon adopted by William Morris at Cowley (Oxford) and by Herbert Austin at Longbridge (Birmingham). By 1932 the British motor industry was second only to that of the USA. Hundreds of different components (tyres, windows, headlights, paint, upholstery) were made in separate factories, then put together in the motor vehicle assembly plant. Access to good road and rail links was more important than a site near a coalfield or steel works.

Halted by the Second World War, British production grew rapidly again after 1945. So too did that of other European countries, and quite soon they were outstripping the UK: Germany in 1956, France in 1961 and Italy in 1970. The British motor industry reached its peak in 1972; since then it has declined in the face of foreign competition.

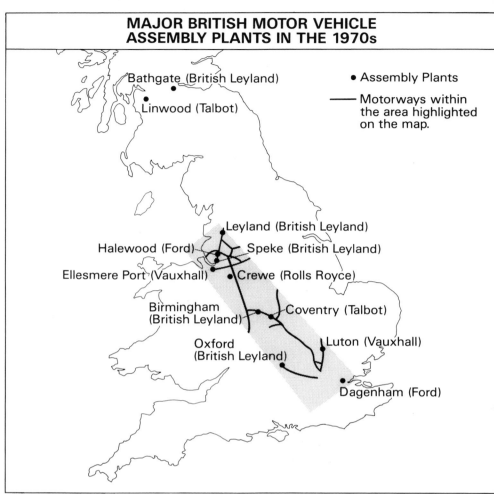

MAJOR BRITISH MOTOR VEHICLE ASSEMBLY PLANTS IN THE 1970s

Bathgate (British Leyland)
Linwood (Talbot)
• Assembly Plants
— Motorways within the area highlighted on the map.
Leyland (British Leyland)
Halewood (Ford)
Speke (British Leyland)
Ellesmere Port (Vauxhall)
Crewe (Rolls Royce)
Birmingham (British Leyland)
Coventry (Talbot)
Oxford (British Leyland)
Luton (Vauxhall)
Dagenham (Ford)

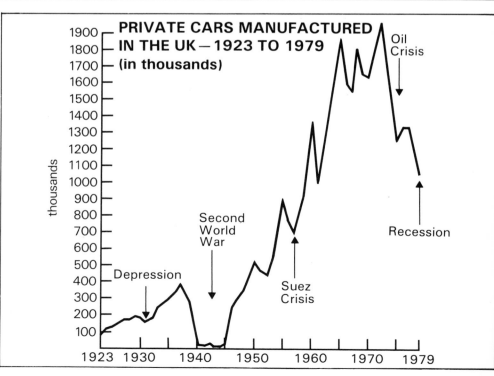

PRIVATE CARS MANUFACTURED IN THE UK – 1923 TO 1979 (in thousands)

Depression
Second World War
Suez Crisis
Oil Crisis
Recession

NEW SOURCES OF POWER

from the Frigg gasfield

Dounreay

Piper Claymore, Tartan

Forties and others

Ekofisk and others

Torness

Hunterston

Chapelcross

Windscale
Calder Hall

Hartlepool

Heysham

Rough
West Sole
Viking
Indefatigable
Leman Bank

Wylfa

Stanlow

Trawsfynd

Sizewell

Milford Haven

Berkeley
Oldbury

Shellhaven
Bradwell

Isle of Grain

Hinkley Point

Dungeness

Fawley

Winfrith

Gasfields   Oilfields   • Nuclear power stations

····· Pipeline   —— Pipeline   ○ Major oil refineries

Power

Few industries now need to be near a coalfield, since most run on electricity, gas or oil. Until recently the coal-mining industry had little to fear, because large supplies of coal were needed to produce gas and electricity. Today, however, Britain has acquired new sources of energy, thanks to the development of nuclear power and hydro-electric power, and the discovery of North Sea oil and natural gas in the 1960s. The UK is one of the few industrial nations to be self-sufficient in oil, coal and gas.

Factors which were vital to the siting of new industries in the Industrial Revolution are now relatively unimportant. There are new reasons why industries have been attracted to different parts of Britain. Since the war, it has been government policy to encourage industrialists to build new factories in Special Development Areas, where there is high unemployment. Most of these are places which used to be important centres for industries like coal-mining and shipbuilding. Cheap loans, low labour costs, the availability of building sites on industrial estates, and good access to London, motorways and container ports are also important considerations.

?????????????????

Imagine you are one of the great industrialists of the past (such as James Watt or Henry Bessemer). Write an article for a newspaper describing your impressions of industry in modern Britain.

Roads

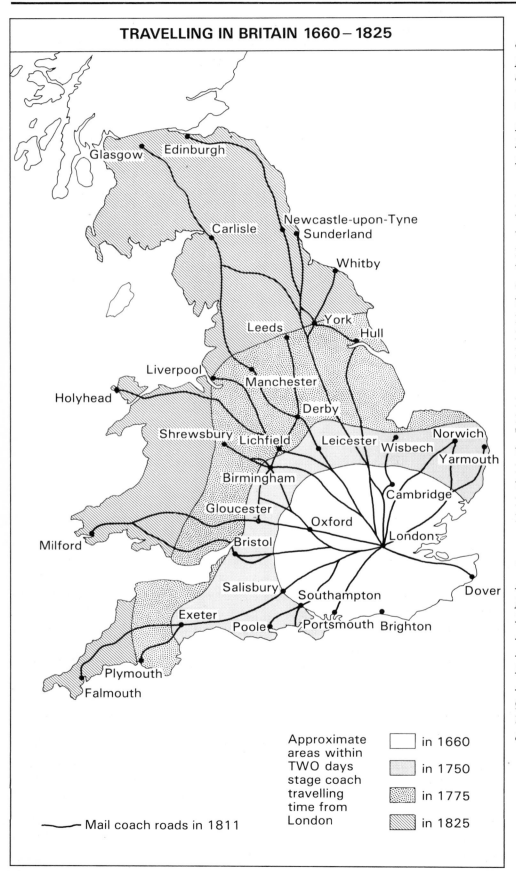

TRAVELLING IN BRITAIN 1660–1825

Glasgow
Edinburgh
Carlisle
Newcastle-upon-Tyne
Sunderland
Whitby
Leeds
York
Hull
Liverpool
Manchester
Holyhead
Derby
Shrewsbury
Lichfield
Leicester
Norwich
Wisbech
Yarmouth
Birmingham
Cambridge
Gloucester
Oxford
London
Milford
Bristol
Salisbury
Southampton
Dover
Exeter
Portsmouth
Brighton
Poole
Plymouth
Falmouth

Approximate
areas within
TWO days
stage coach
travelling
time from
London

in 1660
in 1750
in 1775
in 1825

Mail coach roads in 1811

'There was never a more astonishing revolution accomplished in the internal system of any country, than has been seen within a few years in England. The carriage of grain and coals is in general conducted with little more than half the horses which it formerly was.'

1767 *Report on Roads*

Before 1700 most roads in Britain were very bad. In winter they were often muddy, with deep ruts and potholes. Better roads were badly needed in the eighteenth century because the towns were growing fast and many industries were expanding. More and more people found they needed to visit different parts of the country.

Turnpike Trusts were set up from 1700 onwards to build new roads (called *turnpikes*). The Trusts collected tolls from travellers to pay for these new roads and to repair and improve them. At first, the standard of the roads varied, and many were not much better than the old ones.

'Near Newcastle-under-Lyme. Turnpike. As narrow as can be conceived, and cut into perpetual holes; a more dreadful road cannot be imagined.
Brentford to London turnpike. Excellent. But much too narrow for such vast traffic.
Kendal to Windermere. As good, firm, level a road as any in the world, I nowhere remember a better.'

Arthur Young 1770

TURNPIKES

ADVANTAGES	DISADVANTAGES
1 Better road surfaces made travel faster and transport cheaper. **2** More comfortable journeys. **3** Faster mail service. **4** Quicker to get cattle and sheep to market on good roads.	**1** Some turnpikes badly built or kept in a poor state of repair. **2** Few skilled road builders at first. **3** Not a planned system of roads; so on a journey one stretch of turnpike might be excellent and another terrible.

GROWTH OF THE TURNPIKE ROAD SYSTEM

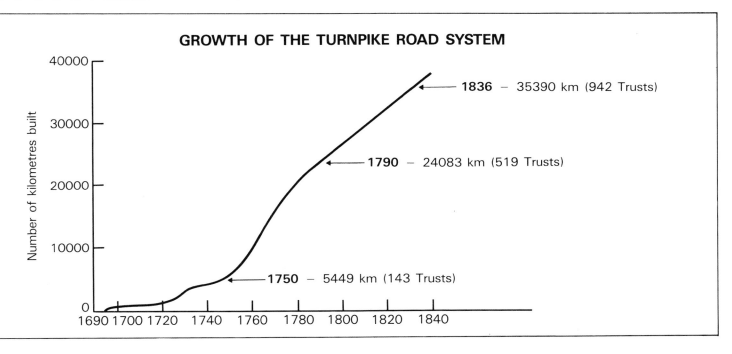

1836 — 35390 km (942 Trusts)

1790 — 24083 km (519 Trusts)

1750 — 5449 km (143 Trusts)

By the 1800s the efforts of skilled road engineers like John Metcalf (1717–1810), Thomas Telford (1757–1834) and John McAdam (1756–1836) had brought great improvements. Journey times were drastically cut. In 1734 the journey from London to Edinburgh took 12 days. By 1762 this time had been cut to under four days and by 1825 it took only 40 hours. These fast times were possible because the road surfaces were smooth and there were many coaching inns and stables. At every stage of a journey (i.e. about 15 km) a coach pulled into the yard of an inn for a fresh team of horses. In 1784 mail coaches were introduced to speed up delivery of the post. These carried fewer passengers, kept to strict time schedules, and carried an armed guard.

'The night and the snow came on together . . . there was no sound to be heard but the howling of the wind, for the noise of the wheels and the tread of the horses' feet were rendered inaudible by the thick coating of snow which covered the ground. The passengers wrapped themselves more closely in their coats and cloaks, and leaving the light and warmth of the town behind them, pillowed themselves against the luggage and prepared, with many half-suppressed moans, again to encounter the piercing blast which swept across the open country.'

Charles Dickens
Nicholas Nickleby

??????????????????????????????

1 Imagine you are an old passenger on a stage coach from London to Edinburgh in about 1811. Describe the changes in road travel which have occurred since your last visit in 1750.
2 What new developments and improvements help to explain why journey times were drastically shortened between 1760 and 1830?

Canals

By 1700 there were already about 2000 km of navigable inland waterways in Britain. Many rivers had been straightened or artificially deepened to make them suitable for navigation by boats.

In 1761 James Brindley designed and constructed the Bridgewater Canal. This revolutionised canal building in Britain. It was spectacular in appearance, with a splendid stone *aqueduct* which carried the canal over the River Irwell. One writer wrote:

'This navigation begins at the foot of some hills, in which the duke's coals are dug, from whence a canal is dug through rocks which daylight never enters . . . I saw the navigation carried sometimes over public roads, and in some places over bogs, but generally by the side of hills.'

The canal halved the cost of carrying coal from Worsley Colliery to Manchester. Other industrialists were impressed by this. Brindley was soon commissioned to design and build the Trent and Mersey Canal between the Trent navigation system and the River Mersey and Bridgewater Canal, thus linking the North and Irish Seas. This is why it was called the Grand Trunk Canal – because it was hoped it would sprout many branch canals. Josiah Wedgwood, the pottery manufacturer, played a large part in promoting the construction of this canal, which later enabled him to bring kaolin from Cornwall and other heavy raw materials to his pottery works at Etruria, near Stoke-on-Trent.

John Rennie and Thomas Telford were other canal builders who helped to construct the 6500 km of navigable waterways which criss-crossed Britain by 1830.

PROBLEMS FOR THE CANAL BUILDERS

1 The course of a new canal had to be carefully marked out and the land purchased—sometimes compulsorily.
2 Large numbers of workmen had to be carefully organised to dig the 'navigation' as it was called. This was why they were called *navvies*. Many travelled from one site to another in search of work.
3 The canal had to have a regular and reliable source of water.
4 The canal banks and bed had to be covered with clay to stop the water being absorbed by the soil underneath.
5 Since it cut across existing rivers, streams, roads and paths, many bridges had to be built.
6 The canal had to be absolutely level; hills and uneven land created many problems. Cuttings had to be made and embankments built. Sometimes aqueducts or tunnels were constructed. If these methods of keeping the canal level were not feasible then a series of locks had to be constructed to lift boats from one level to the next.

CANALS	
ADVANTAGES	**DISADVANTAGES**
1 Enabled manufacturers to move heavy loads of raw materials, coal and manufactured goods to and from their factories. **2** By 1830 few parts of England and Wales were more than 25 km from a canal or navigable river. **3** Transport of heavy goods was much cheaper by canal than by road.	**1** The volume of trade on many canals didn't repay the cost of building them. **2** The depth and width of the canals varied. This made it difficult sometimes to ship a large load from one end of the country to the other. **3** Canal transport was very slow. **4** Canals had to be regularly maintained to stop water leaking away, and to repair the damage done to canal banks.

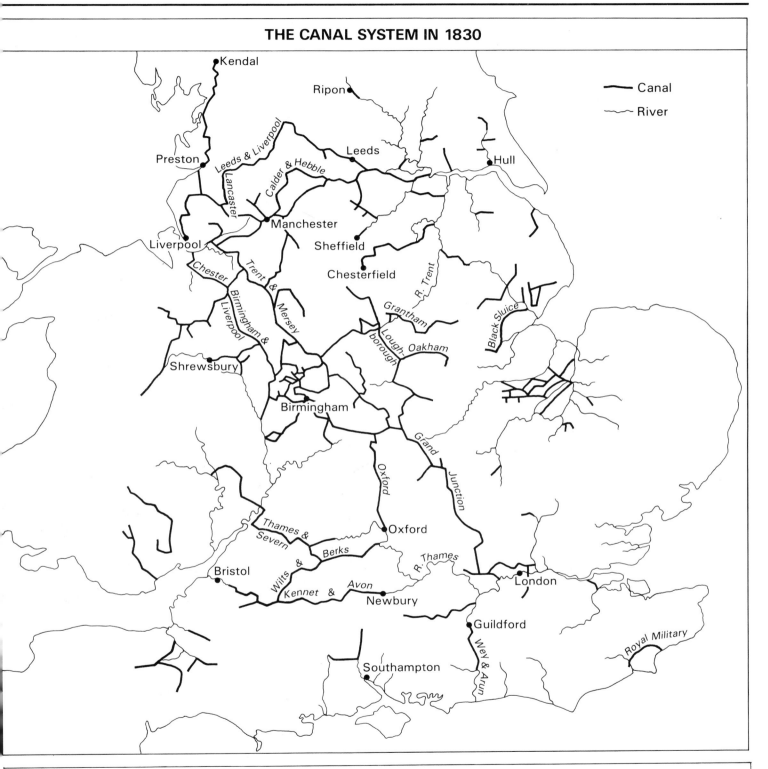

THE CANAL SYSTEM IN 1830

Canal
River

Kendal
Ripon
Preston
Leeds & Liverpool
Lancaster
Calder & Hebble
Leeds
Hull
Manchester
Liverpool
Sheffield
Chester
Trent & Mersey
Chesterfield
R. Trent
Birmingham & Liverpool
Grantham
Black Sluice
Shrewsbury
Lough-borough
Oakham
Birmingham
Grand Junction
Oxford
Thames & Severn
Oxford
Berks
R. Thames
Bristol
Wilts &
Kennet &
Avon
Newbury
London
Guildford
Wey & Arun
Royal Military
Southampton

???

1 Why were a large number of canals built in England in the eighteenth and nineteenth centuries? What benefits did they bring? What were their weaknesses?

2 Look carefully at the picture which contrasts canal and river transport in the middle of the eighteenth century. Which canal is shown? Why was it important? What advantages did a canal have compared with a river?

The Coming of the Railway

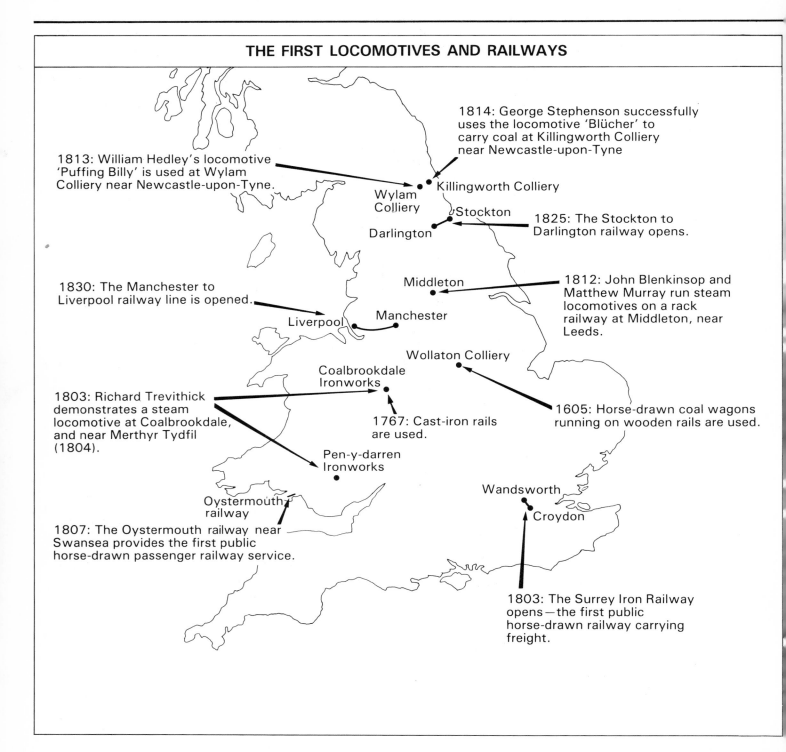

THE FIRST LOCOMOTIVES AND RAILWAYS

1814: George Stephenson successfully uses the locomotive 'Blücher' to carry coal at Killingworth Colliery near Newcastle-upon-Tyne

1813: William Hedley's locomotive 'Puffing Billy' is used at Wylam Colliery near Newcastle-upon-Tyne.

Killingworth Colliery

Wylam Colliery

Stockton

1825: The Stockton to Darlington railway opens.

Darlington

Middleton

1830: The Manchester to Liverpool railway line is opened.

1812: John Blenkinsop and Matthew Murray run steam locomotives on a rack railway at Middleton, near Leeds.

Liverpool   Manchester

Wollaton Colliery

Coalbrookdale Ironworks

1803: Richard Trevithick demonstrates a steam locomotive at Coalbrookdale, and near Merthyr Tydfil (1804).

1767: Cast-iron rails are used.

1605: Horse-drawn coal wagons running on wooden rails are used.

Pen-y-darren Ironworks

Wandsworth

Oystermouth railway

Croydon

1807: The Oystermouth railway near Swansea provides the first public horse-drawn passenger railway service.

1803: The Surrey Iron Railway opens—the first public horse-drawn railway carrying freight.

On 15 September 1830 the opening of the Manchester to Liverpool railway began a process which was to transform Britain and the world. Within twenty years a network of railway lines covered most parts of England and stretched into Wales and Scotland.

?????????????????????????????

1 What do you think were the *five* most significant events in the origin and development of the UK railway system up to 1850?
2 Imagine you were the engineer in charge of building the railway line closest to your school. Describe the problems you think you would have had to overcome and explain how they might have been solved.

PROBLEMS WHICH FACED THE RAILWAY COMPANIES AND THEIR ENGINEERS

Opposition from canal owners who feared competition from the railway — also from stage-coach proprietors, owners of coaching inns and turnpike trusts.

Many railway lines were duplicated when rival companies competed with each other.

Many accidents — drivers and signalmen were often tired when they should have been alert, because they worked long hours.

Building embankments, viaducts and bridges across rivers, roads, canals or other railways.

Digging tunnels and cuttings through hills and slopes, sometimes through very tough rock.

Some landowners refused to sell their land; others made large profits out of the railway companies.

Opposition from farmers and land owners who said the sparks would set their fields on fire; the noise would frighten their animals; the lines would destroy hunting . . .

TIME LINE

The Coming of the Railway

1821 Colliery owners in the Darlington area ask George Stephenson to build a railway from Stockton to Darlington to carry coal. The 43 km railway opens in 1825 with a trainload of passengers but is used primarily for freight traffic (pulled by Stephenson's engine 'Locomotion'). Passengers are still carried in horse-drawn trains.

1826 George Stephenson and his son Robert start to build a railway linking the large northern cities of Manchester and Liverpool.

1830 The Manchester to Liverpool railway is opened. It soon proves a success. By 1832 only one stage coach service is left between the two cities instead of the 29 before the railway was built. Other railways are planned, such as one between London and Birmingham, but they meet fierce resistance from coach and canal owners, Turnpike Trusts and landowners.

1833 Isambard Kingdom Brunel becomes chief engineer to the Great Western Railway. He uses a 2.1 metre gauge (width) for his railway track, unlike the 1.4 metre gauge used by most of the other railway engineers. His GWR line from London to Bristol opens in 1841.

1837 The Grand Junction (Birmingham to Warrington) Railway is opened and links up with the Manchester to Liverpool Railway. George

Hudson, 'The Railway King', becomes Chairman of the York and North Midland Railway and soon controls over 1600 km of track by merging different railways into one big company.

1838 The London to Birmingham Railway opens.

1840s Cheap railway excursion trains run for the first time. A boom period of 'railway mania' begins. Many companies go bust because railways duplicate existing services. Many are inadequately staffed and accidents are common.

1846 The Gauges Act makes the 1.4 metre gauge the national standard for all future railways to enable easy movement of trains from one company's lines to another's.

1921 The Railway Act organises the railway system into four great railway companies—LMS (London, Midland and Scottish), LNER (London and North Eastern Railway), GWR (Great Western Railway) and SR (Southern Railway)—instead of over 100 separate companies.

1947 The railway companies are nationalised and become one large state railway system from 1 January 1948—British Railways (changed to British Rail in 1964).

1962 The Beeching Plan recommends closure of many non-profit-making rural lines and leads to the closure of over 8000 km of track.

The Coming of the Railway: Effects

THE COMING OF THE RAILWAY: EFFECTS

Economic Effects

Industry:
1 It gave a huge boost to the coal-mining industry (since coal was the fuel used by steam engines). It provided the iron and steel industry with a large new market for railway lines, locomotives and rolling stock. When other countries built railways they naturally looked for help, equipment and fuel from the pioneers—Britain.
2 It enabled manufacturers to use raw materials from distant parts of the country and to send their products in return to all parts of Britain. This made mass-production possible and encouraged competition.

Employment:
Up to 250 000 labourers built the new railway lines and over 100 000 workers were employed on the railways.

Other forms of transport:
1 It killed the stage and mail coach services, since they charged four or five times more than the railways and took two to three times as long.
2 It caused a decline in canal trade (but only slowly, since water-borne freight charges were low).

Growth of towns:
1 New buildings grew up near the railway stations, such as station hotels, public houses and shops. At the same time many houses were pulled down to make way for the railways and stations.
2 New towns, like Crewe and Swindon, grew up at railway junctions because these were the best places to build railway engineering works to service the locomotives and railway carriages.
3 People could shop in the great cities instead of relying entirely on their local shopping centres.
4 People could now afford to live at a distance from their places of work. For example, rich commuters lived in Blackpool and travelled by train to Manchester every day. City suburbs began to spread outwards as many ordinary people lived away from the centre.
5 The railway companies helped seaside resorts to grow. Cleethorpes and Skegness owed their existence to the railway.

Farming:
The railways helped farmers to send milk and other perishable foods to London and the other large cities.

Social Effects

Countryside:
The railways altered the appearance of the landscape. Cuttings and embankments scarred the open country, steam and smoke polluted the air and blackened buildings. They created obstacles to free movement of people, animals and machines.

Holidays:
The new seaside resorts grew rapidly as ordinary working people found they were able to afford a cheap day excursion to the sea once or twice a year. Huge swarming crowds thronged the promenades and piers on bank holidays.

Opening people's eyes:
Before the coming of the railways only the well-to-do had been able to afford to travel by stage or mail coach or private carriage. The railways gave many poorer people the opportunity to travel. In 1851 over six million people (a third of the population) attended the Great Exhibition at Crystal Palace in London. They flocked to London in special cheap day excursion trains.

Everyday life:
Many more children could travel to distant public schools. It became easier to send large numbers of soldiers from one part of the country to another. Politicians, school inspectors, health inspectors, touring actors, sports teams and many others could travel easily throughout Britain.

Communications:
London newspapers and magazines could be sent to all parts of the country. The postal service also became more efficient, since letters and parcels could be sent overnight and delivered the following day.

THE BRITISH RAILWAY SYSTEM

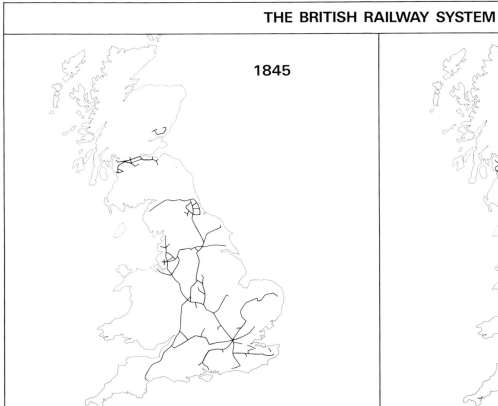

1845

1851

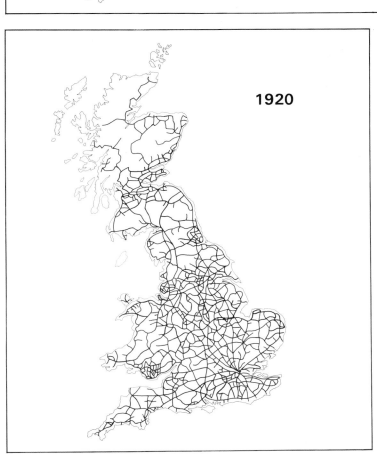

1920

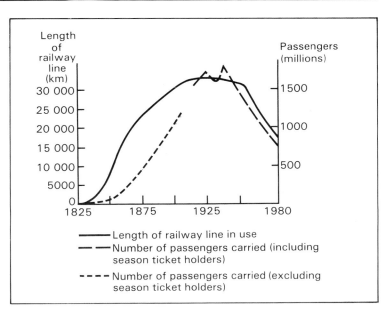

Length of railway line in use

Number of passengers carried (including season ticket holders)

Number of passengers carried (excluding season ticket holders)

??????????????????????????????

1. Compare the maps on these pages. How do they relate to the graphs showing numbers of passengers carried and length of railway line in use?
2. Write an account of the social and economic consequences of building a railway system in the middle of the nineteenth century.

Ships

In 1802 the 'Charlotte Dundas', powered by a single paddle wheel, successfully pulled two barges along the Forth and Clyde canal, in the teeth of a gale. This was something a sailing ship couldn't do within the narrow confines of a canal. But the steamer's wash damaged the canal's banks and it wasn't until 1812 that the first steamboat passenger service opened in Britain, with Henry Bell's 'Comet' on the Clyde.

Soon many other small steam-powered paddle boats were carrying cargo and passengers on short journeys around the coast or across the English Channel. Another innovation at this time was the steamer or sailing ship built with a wooden hull covered with iron plates (ironclads). Later ships had an iron hull.

SAIL VERSUS STEAM

1 Britain had used up most of her good shipbuilding timber (oak).
2 Wooden ships were much more likely to be damaged in bad weather.
3 Sailing ships were difficult to navigate in a confined space, unlike paddle steamers which could be easily manoeuvred.
4 Sailing ships were at the mercy of tides, waves and winds.
5 Sailing ships were unable to sail in a straight line, since they had to tack from side to side when sailing into the wind.
6 Very long wooden ships were not rigid enough to withstand a battering in high seas.

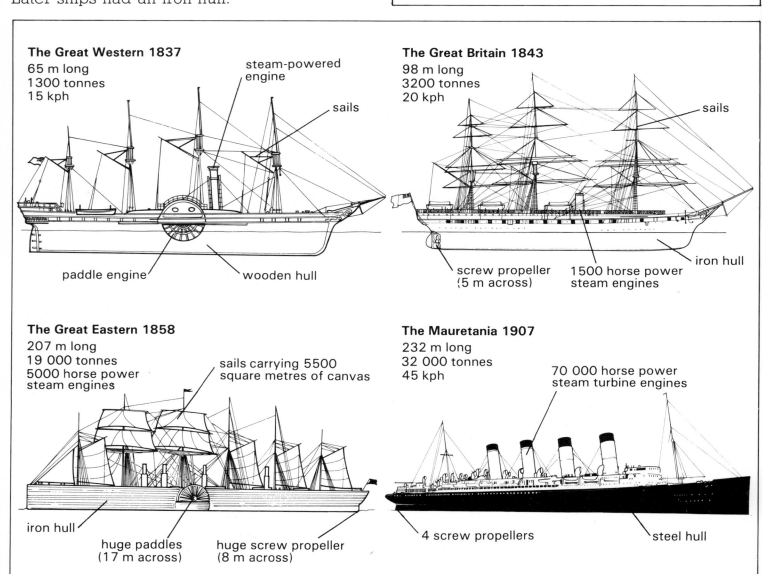

The Great Western 1837
65 m long
1300 tonnes
15 kph

steam-powered engine

sails

paddle engine

wooden hull

The Great Britain 1843
98 m long
3200 tonnes
20 kph

sails

screw propeller (5 m across)

1500 horse power steam engines

iron hull

The Great Eastern 1858
207 m long
19 000 tonnes
5000 horse power steam engines

sails carrying 5500 square metres of canvas

iron hull

huge paddles (17 m across)

huge screw propeller (8 m across)

The Mauretania 1907
232 m long
32 000 tonnes
45 kph

70 000 horse power steam turbine engines

4 screw propellers

steel hull

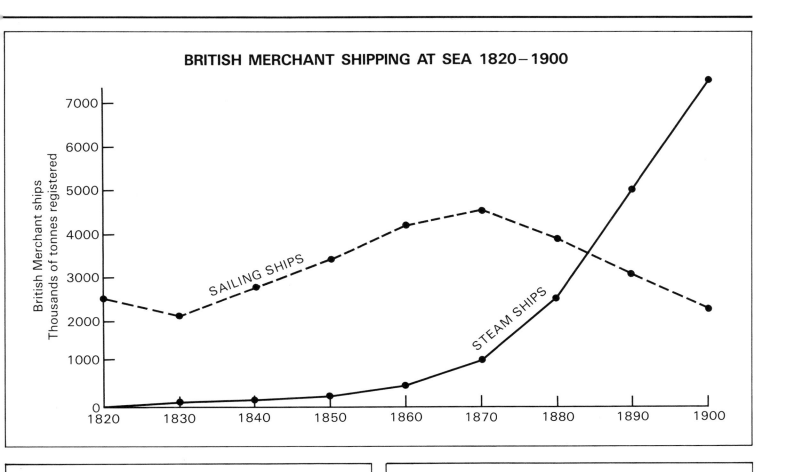

BRITISH MERCHANT SHIPPING AT SEA 1820—1900

British Merchant ships Thousands of tonnes registered

SAILING SHIPS

STEAM SHIPS

DISADVANTAGES OF IRON STEAMSHIPS —AND HOW THEY WERE OVERCOME

1 Cost twice as much to build as sailing ships of similar size.
2 Needed fresh water for the boilers—salt water would corrode the metal. Solved when a condenser was invented in 1843 which re-used the steam—cooling it and so turning it back into water.
3 The early paddle engines didn't grip the water in high seas, since a part of the wheel was always out of the water.
4 The first iron ships were easily corroded and soon encrusted with barnacles (they needed regular cleaning, treatment with preservative and paint).
5 Needed huge quantities of coal at first. One cargo boat carried 500 tonnes of coal as fuel but only 200 tonnes of cargo. Bigger ships and more efficient steam engines were needed. In 1843 Brunel's 'Great Britain' became the first iron ship to be driven by a steam-powered screw propeller instead of a paddle engine. In 1854 the invention of the compound engine cut coal consumption by half and increased the space available for passengers or freight. Later steam engines such as the Triple Expansion Engine (1881) and the Steam Turbine (1894) were even more efficient.

EFFECTS OF THE IMPROVEMENTS IN SHIPPING

1 Reduced travelling times drastically; speeded up passenger travel and delivery of overseas mail. Took 15 days to cross the Atlantic in 1840; less than 5 days in 1907.
2 Reduced freight charges drastically—cutting the cost of shipping wheat from North America to Britain from £2 a tonne in the 1860s to about 30p a tonne in 1900.
3 Iron (later steel) steamships were more reliable, safer and more comfortable to travel in than the old sailing ships.
4 Developed overseas trade, opened up export markets for British industry and played a part in the growth and development of Britain's large overseas empire.

??????????????????????????????

1 When did iron steamships take over from wooden sailing ships? Why did it take so long for them to show their supremacy?
2 Write an account of the changes in methods of construction and propulsion of ships in the nineteenth century.

The Coming of the Motor Car

Over the last 90 years, the development of the motor vehicle has dramatically changed daily life in Britain. It made it much easier for people to travel in towns and cities (by bus and car); it made it easier for factories to assemble raw materials and send their goods to customers (by lorry and van); it made it easier for farmers to farm the land (with tractors and implements such as the combine harvester); it enabled town workers to live in the country or at a distance from their places of work; it gave country people the chance to use the facilities and shops of the towns.

SOCIAL AND ECONOMIC EFFECTS OF THE COMING OF THE MOTOR VEHICLE

1 Several million new jobs were created—making cars and car parts, building roads, in the oil industry and factories producing steel, rubber and glass. Also work as bus and lorry drivers, salesmen, traffic police and so on.

2 Made the roads the most important lines of communication again.

3 Led to the decline of the horse-drawn vehicle and the hundreds of thousands of jobs dependent on it, such as horse-bus drivers, grooms, stable owners.

4 Enabled factory owners to build their works anywhere in Britain. Many new factories were built along the roads leading out of London and other major cities and towns in south-eastern England.

5 Allowed people to travel freely and easily to any part of Britain. Houses were built along the main roads (ribbon development) and city suburbs grew.

6 Public transport improved—especially in the country.

7 Public services such as police, district nurses and fire brigades were better.

8 Affected new housing areas (roads and garages); new dual carriageways and motorways in the country *and* cities, flyovers, by-passes, one-way streets, car parks, multi-storey car parks, motels, traffic signs in the towns.

??????????????????????????????

1 Describe the development of the motor vehicle in Britain since 1896. What have been the most important consequences?

2 How do you account for the variations in the two lines shown on the graph?

TIME LINE

1860 J. J. E. Lenoir builds the first reliable internal combustion engine, in France.

1865 The 'Red Flag' Act forces drivers of road vehicles (steam traction engines at that time) to employ a person with a red flag to give warning of their coming; vehicles are not to exceed 6 kph. This Act later prevents motorists using cars in Britain.

1870s French and German engineers develop the petrol engine.

1887 Gottlieb Daimler drives the world's first motor car in Germany. Soon German and French motor cars are being manufactured for sale to the public.

1888 J. B. Dunlop re-invents the pneumatic tyre.

1895 Rudolf Diesel invents the diesel engine.

1896 The 'Red Flag' Act is repealed and motorists celebrate by driving from London to Brighton. F. W. Lanchester makes the first British car.

1900s British manufacturers concentrate on making hand-made luxury cars for the wealthy but Americans mass-produce cheap cars for the ordinary person.

1909 A Road Fund tax is imposed on motor vehicles and on petrol to pay for new roads and road improvements.

1919 After the First World War army lorries are converted to civilian use and road haulage businesses spring up everywhere. Hundreds of private bus companies compete with each other for customers.

1920s Morris and Austin make the first cheap British motor cars and each year the number of cars on the roads increases dramatically.

1926 Traffic lights are introduced.

1930 Road deaths reach 7000 in one year. The Road Traffic Act makes it compulsory for bus drivers to take a driving test and for their vehicles to pass an inspection.

1934 Safety measures are introduced, including 'cats' eyes' in the road and belisha (now zebra) crossings.

1935 Driving tests for all motorists are introduced; also 30 mph (48 kph) speed limits in towns.

1941 Road deaths reach an all-time high during the blackout.

1959 The first motorway (M1) is opened.

1965 The 70 mph (112 kph) speed limit on all roads is introduced.

1983 Safety belts have to be worn by drivers and front-seat passengers.

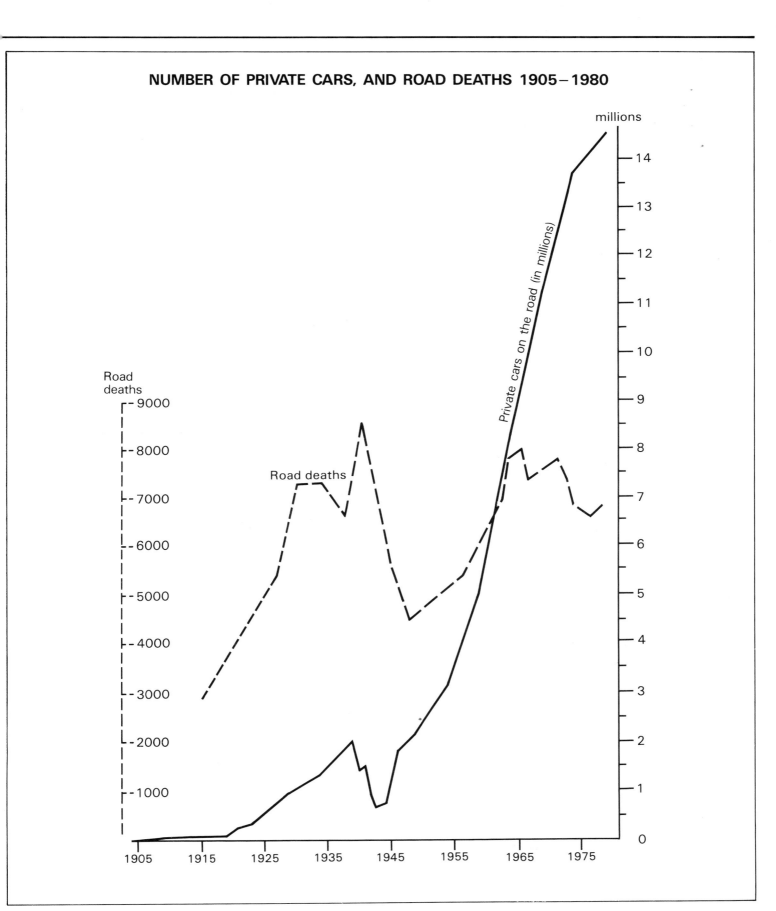

NUMBER OF PRIVATE CARS, AND ROAD DEATHS 1905–1980

Post and Telecommunications

Developments in post and telecommunications have had striking and far-reaching effects. Telephones and computers help people to communicate quickly and easily with friends and colleagues. Television provides 'instant' entertainment and information. In the future, people will need to make fewer journeys by road, rail, ship or air than they do now.

TIME LINE

Date	Development	Effects
1837	William Cooke and Sir Charles Wheatstone invent an electric telegraph which can send messages along wires. In the following year Samuel Morse introduces a simpler system using the Morse code. By 1851 a telegraph cable has been laid across the English Channel—and across the Atlantic by 1866.	Used by the railway companies at first for signalling. Later used to speed up communications. In the past, news of great events only travelled as fast as the fastest form of transport; now news from the Crimean War reached London the day it was sent.
1840	Sir Rowland Hill introduces the penny post. People pay in advance by attaching a postage stamp to their letters—instead of the recipient paying a charge based on the distance the letter has travelled.	Immediately triples the number of letters posted in Britain and reduces the cost of sending a letter from London to Dublin from 16d (7p) to 1d (0.4p).
1876	Alexander Graham Bell, a Scotsman working in the USA, invents the telephone. Later developments include A. B. Strowger's automatic exchange (dial a number) in 1889, the launch of Telstar in 1962 to take telephone calls from Europe to the USA by satellite, and Prestel—the Post Office telephone/television/computer information system.	Soon proves indispensable—Queen Victoria gets a telephone as early as 1877, for instance. Has an incalculable effect in improving the efficiency of businesses, the emergency services, the armed services, and the day to day life of ordinary people.
1894	Guglielmo Marconi experiments with radio waves and in 1895 transmits a radio signal across a distance of 1½ km. In 1897 he sends radio messages across a distance of 20 km, in 1899 across the English Channel, and in 1901 across the Atlantic.	Radio enables messages and warnings to be sent to aircraft and to ships at sea (e.g. the S.O.S. messages from the 'Titanic'). It also brings instant news and entertainment to people living in the most remote parts of the world.
1926	John Logie Baird follows up earlier inventors and demonstrates television for the first time in London. He shows colour pictures two years later. In 1936 the first live television service is started by the BBC.	Television only really catches on after the War, but then its growth is rapid and it causes a decline in cinema attendances and in other forms of entertainment. Its use in the 1970s and 1980s as the focus for video games, video films, home computers and computer information services has further sweeping effects.

Air Travel

TIME LINE

1903 Orville and Wilbur Wright make the first flight in an aeroplane.

1909 Blériot flies across the English Channel.

1914 The aeroplane proves its value in the First World War.

1919 Alcock and Brown fly across the Atlantic. The first passenger air service between London and Paris begins.

1924 Imperial Airways is formed and subsidised by the government. Long distance air routes reach many parts of the Commonwealth.

1932 A regular airline service is opened between England and Australia.

1935 A new company is formed, called British Airways, to run air services between Britain and Europe.

1937 Sir Frank Whittle invents the jet engine.

1940 Imperial Airways and British Airways amalgamate to form BOAC (British Overseas Airways Corporation). Wartime developments greatly advance aircraft design. Stronger and faster aeroplanes are built—better able to cope with prolonged flight and capable of carrying a much larger payload (i.e. passengers and cargo) over twice the distance.

1946 British European Airways (BEA) is formed to operate air services inside the UK and with Europe.

1952 The world's first jet airliner—the Comet—begins a regular BOAC service between London and Johannesburg.

1958 Airliners take more passengers to North America than ocean liners.

1969 The British and French supersonic airliner, Concorde, flies at twice the speed of sound.

1970 The American Boeing 747 Jumbo Jet is introduced.

1972 BOAC and BEA become British Airways.

1976 Concorde goes into service.

Each year British airlines carry about twice as many international passengers as any other country in the world, with the exception of the USA. On internal routes, Britain has only 6 million air passengers compared with over 200 million in the USA and 100 million in the USSR. Because the UK is so small, there is often little significant difference in travelling time from city to city by air, rail or road. This is why the UK has relatively few airports.

One of the most important social effects has been to bring foreign holidays within the reach of ordinary working people. Cheap air travel has opened up the world. Passenger air traffic roughly doubled in the UK between 1948 and 1951, 1951 and 1956, 1956 and 1960, 1960 and 1966, and 1966 and 1975.

?????????????????????????????

1 Describe the development of air transport in the twentieth century.

2 What have been the most important developments in communications in the last 150 years and how have they affected social and economic conditions in the UK?

BRITISH AIR ROUTES UP TO 1939

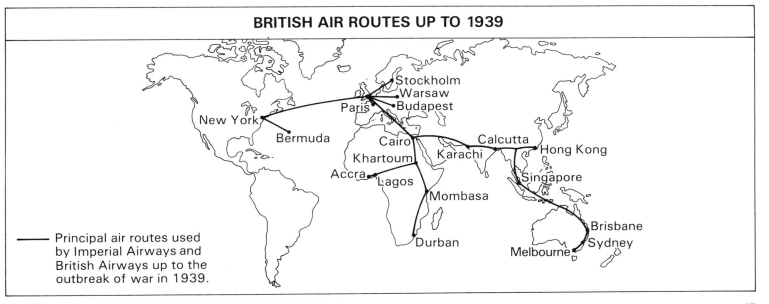

——— Principal air routes used by Imperial Airways and British Airways up to the outbreak of war in 1939.

The Napoleonic Wars brought hardship to ordinary people in Britain. Bread prices rose because foreign wheat couldn't be imported from Europe. Taxes were put on goods to pay the cost of fighting the war. When the war ended in 1815 Government orders to factories for uniforms and weapons were drastically cut. Wages fell and many workers were sacked.

The growing number of unemployed workpeople was swelled by soldiers and sailors returning from the wars. There was no unemployment benefit then, and the price of bread was kept artificially high when the Government brought in the Corn Laws (see page 10).

New machines were threatening the livelihoods of thousands of textile workers. Luddite protesters used hammers to break up stocking frames and power looms. The ringleaders were executed or transported overseas, but this didn't stop other demonstrations and food riots in many parts of Britain.

THE SIX ACTS OF 1819

1 Banned publishers and writers from printing anything that might encourage people to riot or break the law (this was called *seditious libel*).

2 Banned unlawful military drill and weapon training.

3 Gave magistrates the power to search private property for weapons.

4 Banned unlawful political meetings.

5 Speeded up the trial of riot offenders; so that people could see that the law would be rapidly and severely upheld.

6 Put a tax (stamp duty) on newspapers to make them too dear for ordinary people to buy—and so stop the spread of ideas of reform (and revolution).

Peterloo

RIOTS AND DISTURBANCES BETWEEN 1811 AND 1842

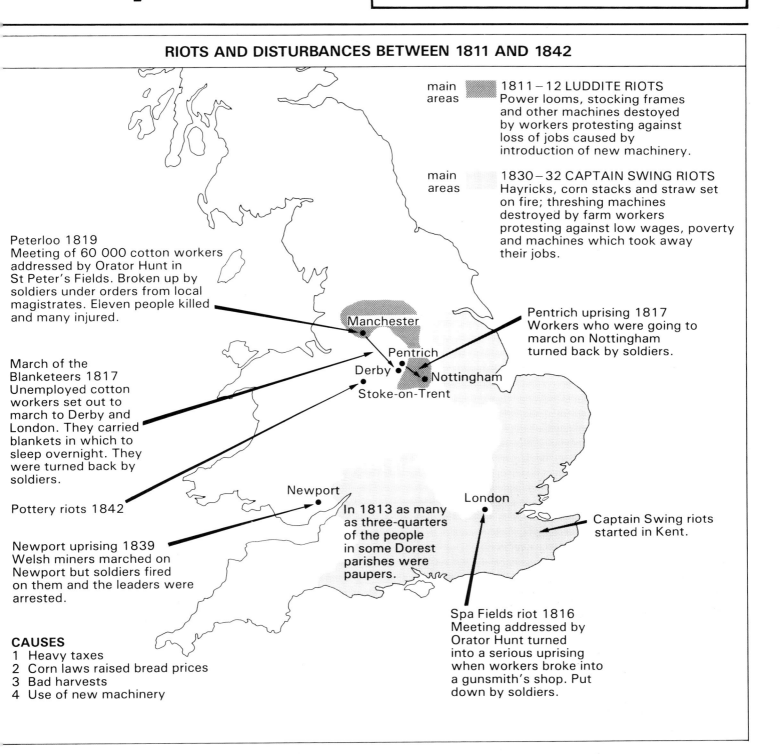

main areas **1811–12 LUDDITE RIOTS**
Power looms, stocking frames and other machines destoyed by workers protesting against loss of jobs caused by introduction of new machinery.

main areas **1830–32 CAPTAIN SWING RIOTS**
Hayricks, corn stacks and straw set on fire; threshing machines destroyed by farm workers protesting against low wages, poverty and machines which took away their jobs.

Peterloo 1819
Meeting of 60 000 cotton workers addressed by Orator Hunt in St Peter's Fields. Broken up by soldiers under orders from local magistrates. Eleven people killed and many injured.

March of the Blanketeers 1817
Unemployed cotton workers set out to march to Derby and London. They carried blankets in which to sleep overnight. They were turned back by soldiers.

Pottery riots 1842

Newport uprising 1839
Welsh miners marched on Newport but soldiers fired on them and the leaders were arrested.

Pentrich uprising 1817
Workers who were going to march on Nottingham turned back by soldiers.

Manchester

Pentrich

Derby

Nottingham

Stoke-on-Trent

Newport

In 1813 as many as three-quarters of the people in some Dorest parishes were paupers.

London

Captain Swing riots started in Kent.

Spa Fields riot 1816
Meeting addressed by Orator Hunt turned into a serious uprising when workers broke into a gunsmith's shop. Put down by soldiers.

CAUSES
1 Heavy taxes
2 Corn laws raised bread prices
3 Bad harvests
4 Use of new machinery

The government feared a revolution (like the one in France thirty years earlier). After Peterloo the Six Acts were passed, which limited the freedom of people to protest. This halted the protest movements for a time, but there were fresh disturbances in 1830–32, 1839 and 1842.

???????????????????????????

1 Why was there so much distress and so many disturbances in the second decade of the nineteenth century (from 1810 to 1820)?
2 Write an imaginary conversation, in 1840, between a Wiltshire farm labourer and a Nottinghamshire textile worker, reminiscing about past disturbances and riots in which they have taken part.

Parliamentary Reform

Before 1832 there was a growing demand from people in the industrial towns for a say in the election of MPs. When the Great Reform Bill was passed in 1832 it didn't give the vote to the working class, many of whom were bitterly opposed to the government. Some people, like Feargus O'Connor, urged revolutionary action, but men like Francis Place and William Lovett sought peaceful means instead. They drew up a People's Charter in 1838, which demanded reforms to make

EFFECTS OF THE 1832 REFORM BILL

Seats in the House of Commons which were *gained* after the Great Reform Bill of 1832 ■

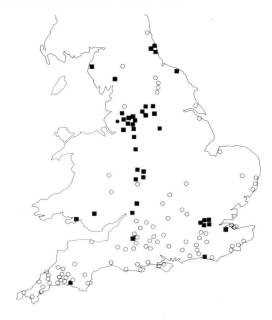

Seats in the House of Commons which were *lost* after the Great Reform Bill of 1832 ○

THE PEOPLE'S CHARTER

1 Equal Representation—the UK should be divided into constituencies with about the same number of voters in each.

2 Universal Suffrage—every man over the age of 21 should have the vote.

3 Annual Parliaments—there should be a general election every year.

4 No Property Qualifications—anyone, rich or poor, should be able to stand for Parliament and there should be no requirement that a candidate must own property.

5 Secret Ballot—each voter should be able to vote in secret.

6 Payment of MPs—all Members of Parliament should be paid £400 a year.

WHO HAD THE VOTE BEFORE 1832

Rotten Boroughs

The Rotten Borough of Old Sarum consisted of a number of open fields in Wiltshire *but* no houses and no permanent inhabitants! It had *seven* voters. It returned *two* Members of Parliament. There were 55 other Rotten Boroughs like Old Sarum. Many were close to each other in Cornwall.

Industrial Towns

The rapidly growing industrial town of Manchester had a population of about 200 000 people. It had *no* voters. It returned *no* Members of Parliament. Birmingham, Leeds, Sheffield and many other large urban areas were not represented in Parliament.

In ENGLAND as a whole only 1 person in every 50 had the vote.

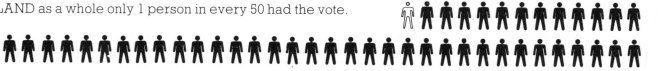

In SCOTLAND it was 1 person in every 500.

In the COUNTIES voters had to be men owning freehold property worth at least £2 a year in rent.
Each county returned *two* Members of Parliament, irrespective of the number of people living in the county.

In the BOROUGHS there were wide differences from town to town. In some you could buy the right to become an MP; in some you had to be a ratepayer in order to vote; in others you had to be a householder, or the owner of a special type of property.

HOW EVERYONE GOT THE VOTE

Date	Act of Parliament	Prime Minister	Terms of Act	Effects
1832	Great Reform Bill	Earl Grey	Abolished 56 Rotten Boroughs. Gave seats in Parliament to new boroughs instead (mainly industrial towns). Gave more seats to the larger counties. Gave the vote to more tenant farmers in the counties. Gave the vote to town property owners, or tenants, in a house worth at least £10 a year in rent.	Gave the vote to the better-off middle classes who had not qualified as electors under the old system. But only to men over the age of 21.
1867	Second Reform Bill	Earl of Derby	Gave the vote to all adult male householders in towns and also to lodgers who paid a rent of at least £10 a year.	Gave the vote to working men who lived in the towns. But only if they were householders or the equivalent.
1872	Ballot Act	Gladstone	Brought in the secret ballot. Prior to this voting had been in public on special stands erected in a square or market place. They were called the *hustings*.	Voters could now vote in secret without being compelled to vote for the candidate favoured by their landlords or employers.
1884	Third Reform Bill	Gladstone	Gave the vote to all householders and lodgers (paying an annual rent of £10) in Britain—provided they were adults and male.	Gave the vote to working men who lived in the country.
1918	Representation of the People Act	Lloyd George	Gave the vote to all adult males (residence was the only qualification) and to women who had reached the age of 30.	Greatly increased the chances of the Labour Party at the polls since all men now had a vote if they were over 21. Gave women the right to vote for the first time.
1928	Equal Franchise Act	Baldwin	Gave the vote to all women over 21 on the same conditions as for men.	Finally gave all women the vote they had been seeking. Every adult now had the vote.
1948	Representation of the People Act	Attlee	Abolished the last cases where people were able to vote twice at an election.	Ensured that each adult had one vote.
1969	Representation of the People Act	Wilson	Reduced the voting age from 21 to 18.	Gave the vote to everyone over the age of 18.

it easier to elect working class MPs. A huge petition was sent to Parliament and when it was rejected there were demonstrations. Further petitions were presented in 1842 and 1848 but these were equally unsuccessful. By this time many workers were better off and support for the Chartists collapsed.

??????????????????????????????

1 Write a conversation between two Chartists in about 1839, in which a supporter of Feargus O'Connor tries to convert a supporter of William Lovett to a more revolutionary method of achieving their demands.
2 Which of the demands made in the Charter were eventually achieved?

The Trade Unions: the Early Years

Before 1800 there had been attempts by work-people to group (or *combine*) together in order to secure better working conditions and higher wages. Most of these were groups of skilled craftsmen working in small workshops. The organisations were usually on a local scale (since long-distance travel was still too expensive for working people) and part of their function was to provide benefits for workers who fell sick.

The growth of the factory system changed all this. It meant that large numbers of workers, sharing the same grievances, often worked under the same roof and for the same employer. When the railway system began to offer cheap travel to any part of the British Isles (see pages 38–41) it paved the way for the formation of national unions of workers in each of the main industries.

?????????????????????????????

1 Explain the importance of the Tolpuddle Martyrs in the history of the early trade union movement.
2 Why did the employers (and the Government) try to stop the spread of trade unions in the early years of the nineteenth century? Why were they afraid?

The Tolpuddle Protest meeting of the Grand National Consolidated Trades Union in 1834

LANDMARKS IN TRADE UNION HISTORY: THE EARLY YEARS

1799–1800 COMBINATION ACTS make trade unions illegal. They have to meet in secret.

1824–1825 REPEAL OF THE COMBINATION ACTS. Trade unions are made legal again. But the new laws severely limit trade union operations and make it possible for strikers to be prosecuted under certain conditions. A number of unions are formed, and there are many strikes. Most collapse because the workers are too poor to hold out for long.

1833 THE GRAND NATIONAL CONSOLIDATED TRADES UNION is founded by Robert Owen to stand up for the rights of workers in many different industries. It soon has well over half a million members and Owen hopes that the Union can use its strength to win higher wages and better working conditions. But the Union lacks funds and is badly organised. Employers employ *blackleg* (non-union) labour during strikes, and starve workers into submission.

1834 THE CASE OF THE TOLPUDDLE MARTYRS (see opposite). The Grand National Consolidated Trades Union organises a protest but it has no immediate effect and the Union soon collapses.

THE TOLPUDDLE MARTYRS

1834. George Loveless, a farm labourer and Methodist preacher, starts a trade union — the Friendly Society of Agricultural Labourers — in the small Dorset village of Tolpuddle.

Farmworkers' wages in Tolpuddle are being cut from 7/- (35p) a week to 6/- (30p). Loveless and his brother James form the Union to keep wages at their previous level.

When each new member is enrolled into the Society he is blindfolded and has to swear an oath on the Bible not to tell anyone about the Society's meetings. Oaths of loyalty, like this, have long been common in friendly societies.

The formation of the Union alarms the authorities but trade unions are not illegal. However they hear about the oath of secrecy and a constable is sent to arrest George Loveless and five other members of the Society.

At Dorchester Assizes the six men are charged with taking an illegal oath. They argue that the law against oaths only applies to the armed services but the Judge finds them guilty.

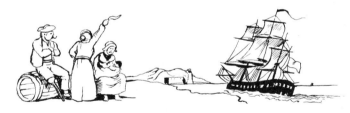

The Judge sentences them to seven years transportation. Two are sent to Tasmania and four to Botany Bay in Australia.

The news shocks working-class leaders and a huge demonstration is organised by the Grand National Consolidated Trades Union. MPs take up the case and put pressure on the Government to intervene.

In 1836 the six men are pardoned and return home to England in 1838. Their experience deters many others from joining a union.

The Trade Unions: in Victorian Times

After the collapse of the Grand National Consolidated Trades Union, skilled craft workers formed *new model unions*. It was largely through their efforts that trade union law changed in the 1870s. Unskilled workers had to wait much longer before their working conditions were improved through trade union action. By 1900 trade union membership had increased, but there were serious disagreements between the craft workers on the one hand and the unskilled workers on the other.

LANDMARKS IN TRADE UNION HISTORY: THE NEW MODEL UNIONS

1851 **NEW MODEL UNIONS.** These are craft unions of skilled workers only. Some of their funds are used for the welfare of their members. They are led by moderate trade union leaders who prefer to talk rather than strike. They are successful, since industry is booming.

1860 **THE JUNTA.** The London Trades Council is formed, and soon dominated by the five secretaries of the main craft unions—William Allan (engineers), Robert Applegarth (carpenters), Edwin Coulson (bricklayers), Daniel Guile (ironfounders) and George Odger (shoemakers). They work hard to convince Parliament and the employers that the trade unions are now respectable organisations, caring for their members, and not hotbeds of revolution.

1866 **SHEFFIELD OUTRAGES.** A cutlery worker's house is blown up with gunpowder because he won't join the union. The newspapers and the Government feel that all their worst fears have been justified.

1867 **HORNBY v CLOSE** case. The treasurer of the Boilermakers' Society embezzles the Union's money but the courts say that a trade union is not entitled to the protection of the courts. A Royal Commission looks into trade unions and reports favourably. The Commission's report leads to the 1871 Acts.

1871 **TRADE UNION ACT** gives the unions legal status and protects their funds. **CRIMINAL LAW AMENDMENT ACT** bans all picketing by trade unions. These measures are passed by Gladstone's Liberal Government and although the first is welcomed the second is greeted with dismay.

1875 **CONSPIRACY AND PROTECTION ACT** is passed by Disraeli's Conservative Government and makes peaceful picketing legal once more.

MEMBERSHIP OF UNIONS AFFILIATED TO THE T.U.C.

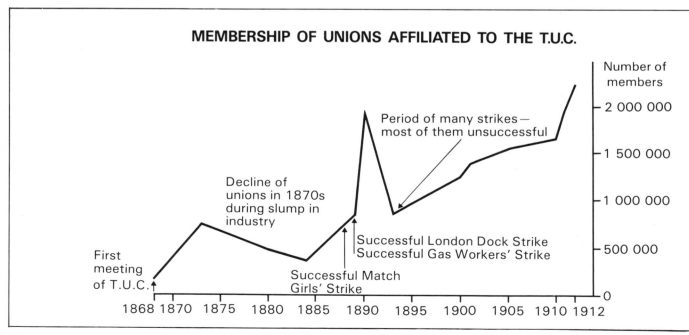

First meeting of T.U.C.

Decline of unions in 1870s during slump in industry

Period of many strikes — most of them unsuccessful

Successful Match Girls' Strike

Successful London Dock Strike
Successful Gas Workers' Strike

Number of members

2 000 000

1 500 000

1 000 000

500 000

0

1868 1870 1875 1880 1885 1890 1895 1900 1905 1910 1912

EVENTS IN TRADE UNION HISTORY 1834 TO 1914

1844, Durham:
Lock-out of miners

1868:
TUC founded
in Manchester

1886, Liverpool:
Seamen's strike

1866: Sheffield
Outrages

1834, Nottingham: Grand
National Consolidated Union
founded

1833–34,
Derby: Lock-out

1911, Llanelly:
Strikers shot dead

1901,
Taff Vale

1888, London:
Matchgirls' strike

1910, Tonypandy:
Troops sent to
protect blackleg
labour

1834,
Tolpuddle

1889, London:
Dock strike

?????????????????

1 Imagine you are a member of the Junta. Write to a new member of your new model union explaining the benefits of joining the union and saying how it has been affected by the Sheffield Outrages, the *Hornby* v. *Close* case and the laws passed in 1871.

2 Look at the graph. Why did the number of trade union members shoot up rapidly between 1884 and 1890?

LANDMARKS IN TRADE UNION HISTORY: THE UNIONS EXPAND

1868 TRADES UNION CONGRESS meets for the first time in Manchester. The T.U.C. is an association of trade unions formed to press for better conditions for trade unionists.

1872 JOSEPH ARCH'S AGRICULTURAL LABOURERS' UNION attempts to organise farmworkers—among the poorest paid workers. He soon has 150 000 members but his union fails in 1874 when a strike collapses and the men go back to work. By 1880 there are few members.

1876 to 1886 SLUMP. A period of depression in industry leads to widespread unemployment and a cut in workers' wages. Support for the unions falls, since they seem to be powerless to improve matters.

1887 FIRST UNSKILLED WORKERS' UNION. Ben Tillet forms the Tea Workers and General Labourers' Union. He and other working class leaders, like John Burns and Keir Hardie want to see the unions using their power more.

1888 MATCHGIRLS' STRIKE. Workers at the Bryant and May works in London go on strike, gain public sympathy, and force their employers to raise their wages.

1889 GASWORKERS' STRIKE successfully reduces working hours in this industry from 12 hours a shift to 8 hours *without* losing any pay.

1889 LONDON DOCKERS' STRIKE led by Ben Tillet forces the employers to recognise the Dockers' Union, to agree to a minimum shift of 4 hours a day, and to pay a standard wage of 6d (2½p) an hour—the Docker's Tanner. (Previously they had worked 2 hour shifts for 5d (2p) an hour.) The dockers win because they have great public support. There are many donations of money, including a generous gift from Australia.

1890 TRADE UNION MEMBERSHIP reaches an all-time high but a renewed slump in trade leads to unemployment, bitter strikes, employers' victories, and disillusioned trade union members.

Only sixteen years after the founding of the Labour Party in 1906, its leader, J. Ramsay MacDonald, became prime minister and formed the first Labour government in 1924. It lasted just a few months, but showed that the Labour Party had leaders capable of running the country. At that time it only had a minority of seats (but it had a majority over the Conservatives with Liberal support). In 1929 Labour became the largest party in the House of Commons.

In 1931 the economic crisis (see pages 60–61) got so bad that a National government was formed from all the parties, with MacDonald as prime minister. However, most Labour MPs opposed the move. At the next election the National government won an overwhelming victory at the expense of the Labour Party.

After the war people in Britain wanted to see changes. They didn't want a return to the Great Depression. In 1945 the Labour Party won a landslide victory, defeating the Conservatives led by Winston Churchill. Labour could now begin a programme to change Britain into a Welfare State (see page 78).

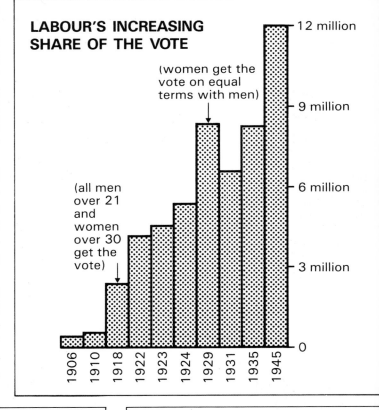

LABOUR'S INCREASING SHARE OF THE VOTE

(women get the vote on equal terms with men)

(all men over 21 and women over 30 get the vote)

12 million
9 million
6 million
3 million
0

1906 1910 1918 1922 1923 1924 1929 1931 1935 1945

---

1 In the middle of the nineteenth century the Liberals and Conservatives failed to tackle the problems which affected the working classes (such as poor housing, unemployment, extreme poverty). MPs were not paid, so only those with private incomes could afford to be elected to Parliament. But they didn't know how working people actually lived.

2 Working men got the vote in 1867 (in the towns) and in 1884 (in the countryside).

3 Trade union leaders wanted to reform trade union laws so they tried to get trade union MPs elected. They formed the Labour Representation League in 1869 to do this, and the first working-class MPs were elected in 1874. They were known as Lib-Labs, because they were associated with the Liberal Party.

ORIGINS OF THE LABOUR PARTY

9 In 1906 29 out of 50 candidates were elected to Parliament and the Labour Representation Committee changed its name to the Labour Party.

4 Some trade union leaders were not satisfied with the Lib-Lab MPs, since they usually voted with the Liberals. They formed the Independent Labour Party (I.L.P.) in 1893. Their leaders were Keir Hardie and John Burns.

8 In 1903 the unions agreed to charge 1d (0.4p) per member, to pay MPs a salary.

7 The Taff Vale decision in 1901 (which threatened to make strikes impossible) convinced doubters in the trade unions that a new left-wing party was necessary. Membership of the new party trebled to nearly 1 million.

6 In 1900 the T.U.C. and the I.L.P. agreed to form a Labour Representation Committee to get members of the *labouring* classes elected. In 1900 two of their 15 candidates were successful.

5 In 1899 the Trades Union Congress passed a motion calling for 'the return of an increased number of labour members to the next parliament.' Trade union support was vital since they had the money to mount an election campaign.

Party

THE COMPOSITION OF PARLIAMENT

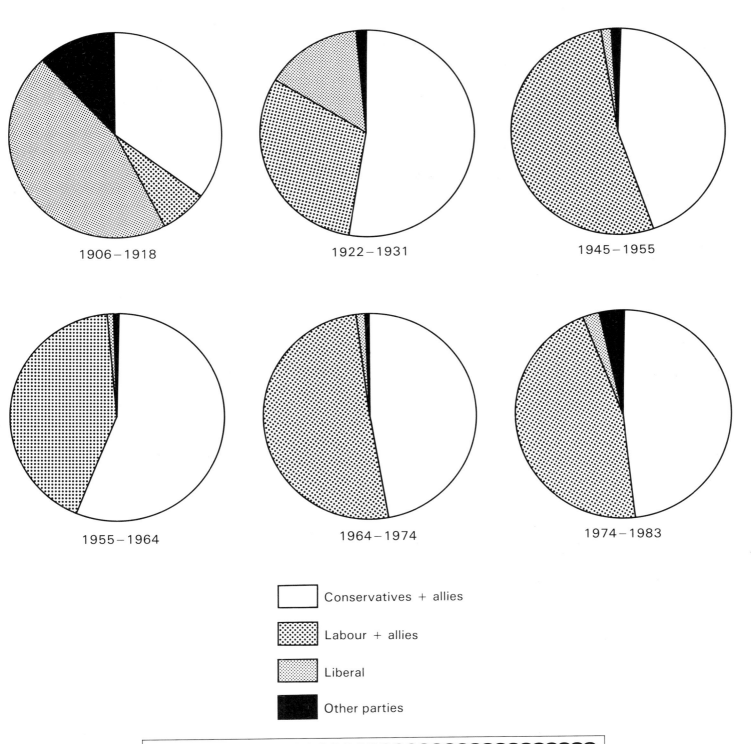

1906–1918

1922–1931

1945–1955

1955–1964

1964–1974

1974–1983

☐ Conservatives + allies

▨ Labour + allies

▦ Liberal

■ Other parties

???
1 What reasons account for the origin and growth of the Labour Party?
2 How important were the unions to the growth of the Labour Party?

The Trade Union Movement in the 20th

LANDMARKS IN TRADE UNION HISTORY: 1900–1930

1901 THE TAFF VALE CASE. A strike in 1900 on the Taff Vale Railway in South Wales results in a court case in which the owners successfully sue the unions for losses sustained during the strike. This decision affects every trade union, since it makes them liable to similar court action if they go on strike.

1906 TRADE DISPUTES ACT. The Liberal Government, supported by Labour MPs, passes a law relieving trade unions of responsibility for any losses incurred by an employer during a strike.

1909 THE OSBORNE JUDGEMENT. A Liberal trade unionist—Walter Osborne—objects to paying part of his Railway Union subscription to a political fund to pay Labour MPs in Parliament. He obtains a court decision which makes it illegal for unions to use members' subscriptions in this way.

1913 TRADE UNION (POLITICAL FUNDS) ACT is passed to allow unions to use funds for political purposes, provided union members who object can *contract out* of paying the part of the subscription going to the Labour Party.

1914 TRIPLE ALLIANCE. Mineworkers, railwaymen and transport workers agree to form an alliance to ensure that future industrial action is effective.

1921 BLACK FRIDAY. Miners striking against proposals to cut their wages are let down by the other members of the Triple Alliance on Friday, 15 April, 1921. The miners eventually have to go back to work.

1926 GENERAL STRIKE (see opposite)

1927 THE TRADE DISPUTES AND TRADE UNION ACT makes general strikes, and sympathy strikes, illegal. It bans the closed shop (where unions insist that all workers in a factory or organisation belong to the same union); clamps down on picketing; bans strikes by the police and some other civil servants; and lays down that in future trade union members will have to *contract in* to any scheme to contribute funds to a political party.

The Great Depression of the early 1930s brought a severe decline in trade. Unemployment rose steeply and wages, as well as unemployment benefit, were cut. Many workers were disillusioned with the trade unions, since they were unable to alleviate hardship or make an effective stand against unemployment. Membership dropped (as you can see from the graph) and only picked up again after the War with the coming of a new Labour Government. The Trade Disputes and Trade Union Act of 1927 was repealed (1946), leaving the unions in the same position as they were in 1926.

In the late 1960s Harold Wilson's Labour Government attempted to reform trade union law and presented a programme for doing so under the title *In Place of Strife*, but trade union opposition killed it. The succeeding Conservative Government, led by Edward Heath, then brought in an Industrial Relations Act (1971) which attempted to clarify relations between unions and employers, but it was again opposed by the unions. Five trade unionists were sent to prison for breaking the law and trade union opposition to the Government was expressed in a coal miners' strike over pay which brought down the Government in 1974. The new Labour Government immediately repealed the Industrial Relations Act.

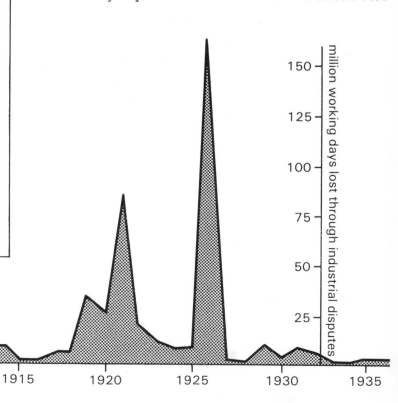

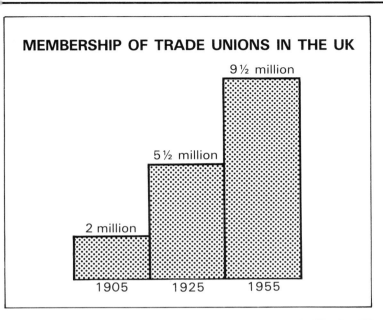

MEMBERSHIP OF TRADE UNIONS IN THE UK

9½ million — 1955
5½ million — 1925
2 million — 1905

% OF UK WORKERS WHO BELONG TO A TRADE UNION

1891, 1921, 1931, 1971

DIARY OF THE GENERAL STRIKE

1925 Mine owners announce wage cuts and a longer working day. The TUC threatens a General Strike if these cuts are implemented. They fear that other employers will also cut wages.

23 July 1925: Red Friday Prime Minister Stanley Baldwin offers to make up miners' wages for a few months, until a Commission can report.

1926 The Commission recommends **1** a cut in miners' wages, **2** an extra hour's work every day. The miners retaliate with the slogan 'Not a penny off the pay. Not a minute on the day.'

1 May 1926 Mine owners lock out the miners and close the pits.

3 May 1926 The TUC calls a General Strike. Government volunteers man essential services and soldiers patrol the streets. Leading trade unionists and Labour politicians fear the consequences if the strike gets out of hand and people are killed. The Government, too, is aware of the possibility of a revolution. Efforts are made behind the scenes to settle the strike, and a number of trade unionists eventually agree to call if off.

12 May 1926 The strike ends. Mineworkers stay out for several months but eventually go back to work, feeling betrayed.

?????????????????????????????

1 How did the following assist or hamper the trade union movement: **a** the Taff Vale decision **b** the Osborne Judgement **c** the Trade Union (Political Funds) Act **d** the Trade Disputes and Trade Union Act?
2 What were the causes and effects of the 1926 General Strike?

WORKING DAYS LOST THROUGH STRIKE ACTION 1893–1980
(in millions)

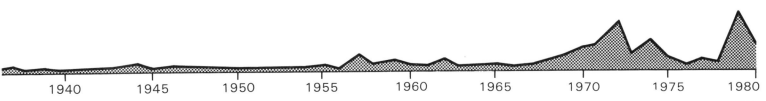

1940   1945   1950   1955   1960   1965   1970   1975   1980

The Great Depression

The Great Depression of the early 1930s was sparked off by the Wall Street Crash in New York in 1929. But unemployment had been a serious problem in Britain ever since the end of the First World War. Many industries were already in serious trouble and prospects for the future didn't look good.

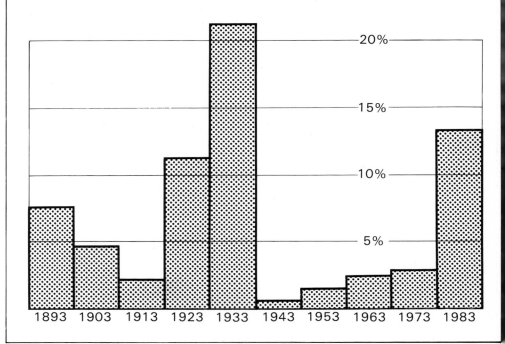

% OF THE WORKFORCE UNEMPLOYED

1893 1903 1913 1923 1933 1943 1953 1963 1973 1983

CAUSES	EFFECTS

CAUSES

1 American manufacturers and farmers had been producing more than they could sell. The boom years up to 1929 had seen Americans borrowing money to buy cars, radios and shares in the expanding industries. Then share prices suddenly fell and many became worthless. Businesses and banks went bankrupt. Unemployment soared. Americans withdrew money they had loaned to countries in Europe.

2 Trade between countries fell off. Many put tariffs (taxes) on foreign imports to make it easier for their own farmers and manufacturers. This particularly affected the UK since it depended for its prosperity on exporting goods and making use of its large merchant shipping fleet.

3 The value of the pound was too high. This meant that British goods were very expensive abroad. Foreign goods were often cheaper. So British manufacturers found it harder to sell their products.

EFFECTS

1 Unemployment in Britain climbed rapidly to nearly three million. Foreigners began to doubt whether the pound would stay at its old high value, so they began to withdraw the money they had deposited in the UK. The Labour government tried to restore their confidence in the pound by borrowing money from abroad. But a loan could only be obtained if they agreed to (**a**) raise taxes (**b**) cut wages of public employees, such as soldiers and teachers (**c**) cut unemployment benefit.

2 The Labour party split in two. MacDonald resigned and formed a new National Government with Conservative and Liberal support. Public employees had their wages cut by about 10%. Unemployment benefit was also cut by 10%, and further reduced if any member of an unemployed person's family had another income. Working people hated the *Means Test* (as it was called), since many an unemployed worker found himself having to ask his children, or his wife, for money.

3 The Depression in world trade meant that fewer ships were needed, not more; so one of the worst-hit industries was the shipbuilding industry.

4 High unemployment meant less money to spend in shops; so many small businesses had to close—making even more people unemployed.

5 The Depression had relatively little effect on people in south-east England, since many new industries were attracted to the London area.

ACTION TO LIFT THE DEPRESSION

1 The Government *devalued the pound* to make British exports cheaper than those of other countries. If MacDonald had done this at the start of the crisis he might not have split the Labour Party.

2 *Import duties* (tariffs) were imposed on some foreign goods to make it cheaper to buy British. Commonwealth goods carried a lower rate of duty; this was called Imperial Preference.

3 *Special Areas* were given advantages to encourage manufacturers to build new factories in the places worst hit by the Depression.

4 Firms were encouraged to join together to make them more efficient and lower their costs. Money was paid by the Government to encourage the shipbuilders to co-operate in building new ocean liners.

5 Money was paid to *farmers* to encourage them to grow more food, since the more British food that was eaten, the less need there would be to buy from abroad.

6 *Interest rates* were lowered to make it easier for firms to borrow money to build new factories.

7 *Rearmament* in the late 1930s also helped to reduce unemployment, since it provided extra jobs in factories making aircraft and weapons.

8 The *trade unions* were powerless to help their members and membership slumped. In October 1936 the Jarrow Crusade of 200 hungry men marched on London, led by the Labour MP Ellen Wilkinson. She called Jarrow 'The town that was murdered' and the march helped to draw public attention to the plight of the unemployed.

UNEMPLOYMENT IN SIX TOWNS IN 1934

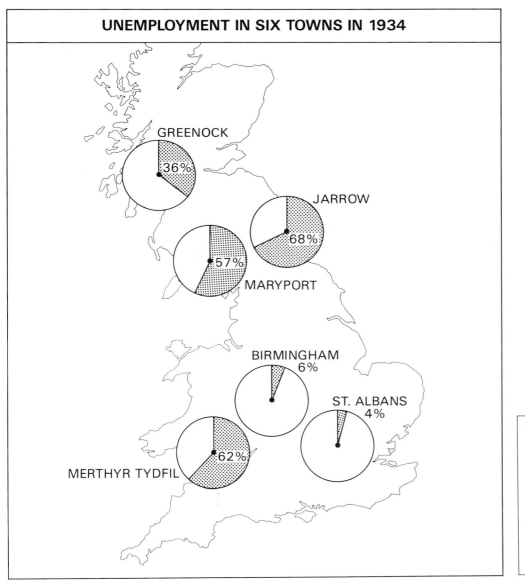

GREENOCK 36%

JARROW 68%

MARYPORT 57%

BIRMINGHAM 6%

ST. ALBANS 4%

MERTHYR TYDFIL 62%

??????????????????

1 How did the Depression come about? Could the Labour government have stopped it having such a devastating effect on the life of the country?

2 What were the effects of the Depression? How did the National Government attempt to solve the problem?

The Suffragette Movement

In the nineteenth century job opportunities for women increased (e.g. as shop assistants, typists and teachers) but they got lower pay than men for doing the same work. Women were admitted to universities and a law was passed giving married women the right to own property in their own names. But it many ways women were treated as second-class citizens. The suffragettes felt that these injustices could only be put right if they had the vote (*suffrage*).

At this time, however, many working men were still without the right to vote, since it was only given to householders and lodgers who paid a certain amount of rent (see page 51). The Liberal government was afraid that if women who owned property in their own right were given the vote they would support the Conservatives.

(see page 51)

????????????????????????????

1 Write an imaginary conversation in 1913 between a suffragette and a Liberal MP in which the former explains and justifies suffragette acts of violence.
2 What steps have been taken in the last hundred years or so, to give women equal rights with men?

TIME LINE

1860s Women's Suffrage Societies are formed to agitate for equal voting rights for women. They get sympathy but very little action.

1903 The WSPU (Women's Social and Political Union) is founded by Mrs Emmeline Pankhurst and her daughters Christabel and Sylvia. They plan protest demonstrations, heckling at meetings, posters and pamphlets.

1907 The movement grows in strength, gaining wide publicity. WSPU branches are formed all over Britain. Suffragettes are arrested by the police.

1908 The protests increase. Suffragettes chain themselves to railings. The first of several private bills to grant votes to women is delayed by the Government.

1909 Some suffragettes break windows and are sent to prison. They go on hunger strike, and since the authorities do not want to have dead suffragettes as martyrs, they are released. Later in the year other suffragettes are not so lucky. They are held down and forcibly fed.

1910 Lady Constance Lytton is sent to gaol, forcibly fed, and later becomes seriously ill. This causes fresh attempts to pass a Conciliation Bill which will grant the vote to women of property. But it is again delayed by the Government.

1912 Suffragettes, frustrated at the lack of progress, smash windows in London's West End. Police and prison brutality is met by even more violence—setting fire to buildings and destroying mail in letter boxes.

1913 Bomb explosions (Lloyd George's house), fires, and cutting telephone wires put pressure on the Government. Reluctant to let women die as a result of hunger strikes, they pass the 'Cat and Mouse' Act (Prisoners' Temporary Discharge for Ill Health Act). When Mrs Pankhurst is sent to prison for three years the violence escalates. On June 4 Emily Wilding Davison receives fatal injuries when she throws herself under the King's horse in the Derby.

1914 Violence continues, with no sign that the Government will agree to Suffragette demands. But soon after war begins in August, a truce is declared. Suffragettes are released from prison and Mrs Pankhurst says *'What is the use of fighting for a vote if we have not got a country to vote in?'*

1914 to 1918 Women effectively prove their right to be treated equally with men by working in hospitals, munitions factories and in the forces.

1918 Women who have reached the age of 30 are given the vote.

1928 Women are given equal voting rights with men.

1960s The women's movement becomes a powerful voice again. The Equal Pay Act (1970) and the Sex Discrimination Act (1975) attempt to eliminate some of the injustices and ensure equal pay for equal work.

THE 'CAT AND MOUSE' ACT

Goes on hunger strike . . .

Suffragette goes to prison . . .

Becomes weak and ill . . .

Recovers her health and is then re-arrested

Is released from prison (because the authorities do not want her to die a martyr) . . .

VOTES FOR WOM

Changes in Distribution of Population

The population of England and Wales grew slowly until about the middle of the eighteenth century and then began to grow more rapidly. It increased by about a third to a half between 1750 and 1800; doubled between 1801 and 1850; and doubled again between 1851 and 1910. This growth was not uniform throughout the British Isles. Scotland and Northern Ireland both lost a lot of people due to emigration overseas or to England. Rural areas lost people to the industrial cities and towns, which grew at a colossal rate. Birmingham's population multiplied by five between 1801 and 1881, and Bradford's grew from 6000 to 194 000 in the same period.

This population expansion put enormous pressures on the towns. Provision of water supply, drainage, sanitation, public transport, food supply,

fire-fighting services and policing, as well as the alleviation of poverty and distress, were just a few of the difficulties which had to be overcome (see page 69). In 1801 only one person in five lived in a town. By 1901 three-quarters of the population were town dwellers.

In the 1930s the depression in the coal-mining, shipbuilding, steel and textile industries of the North and West led to a slower growth rate than in the south-east of England. By contrast, most of the home counties, around London, more than doubled in population between 1932 and 1971. Developments in public transport made it possible for many people to move away from London and commute to work from Surrey, Middlesex and other counties.

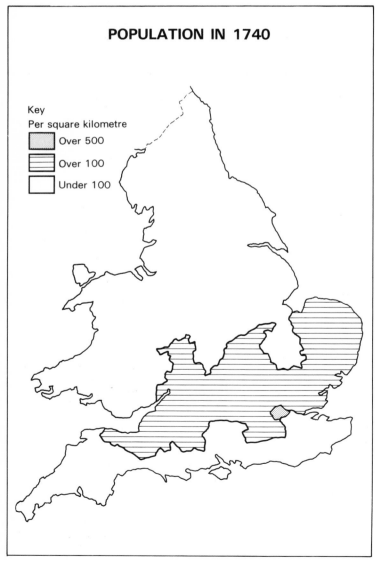

POPULATION IN 1740

Key
Per square kilometre
Over 500
Over 100
Under 100

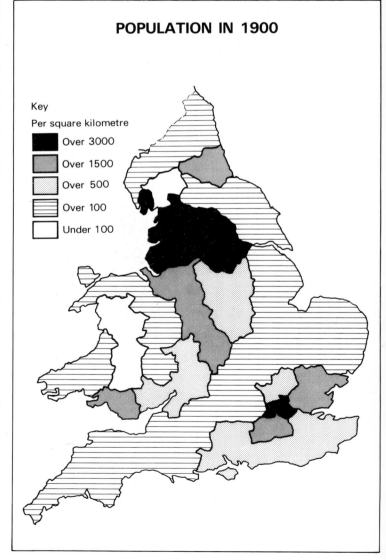

POPULATION IN 1900

Key
Per square kilometre
Over 3000
Over 1500
Over 500
Over 100
Under 100

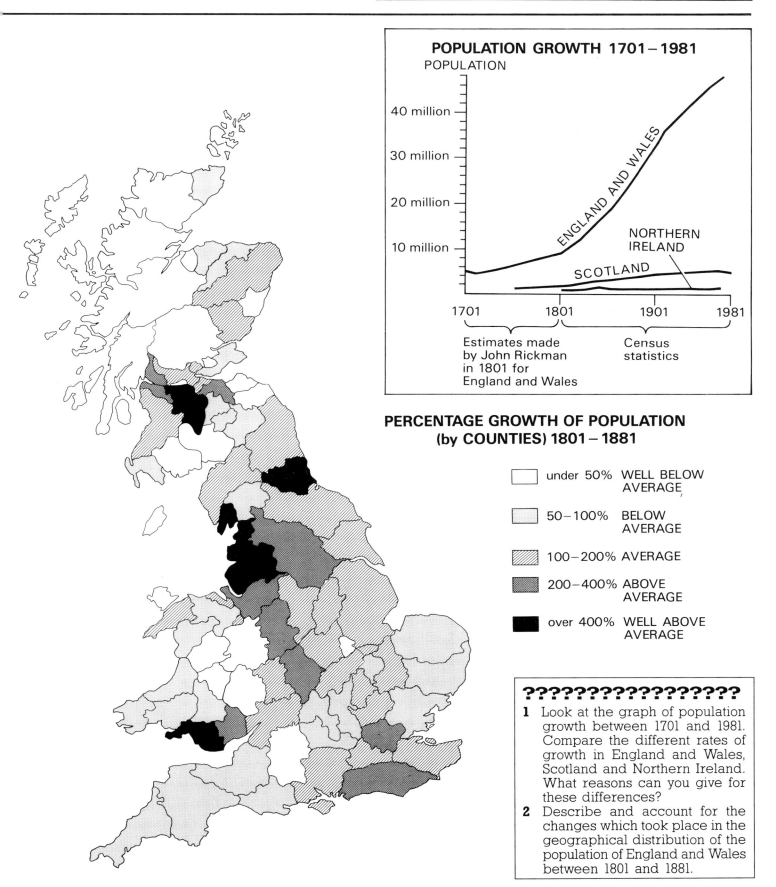

POPULATION GROWTH 1701–1981

POPULATION

40 million

30 million

20 million

10 million

ENGLAND AND WALES

NORTHERN IRELAND

SCOTLAND

1701   1801   1901   1981

Estimates made by John Rickman in 1801 for England and Wales

Census statistics

PERCENTAGE GROWTH OF POPULATION (by COUNTIES) 1801–1881

under 50%   WELL BELOW AVERAGE

50–100%   BELOW AVERAGE

100–200%   AVERAGE

200–400%   ABOVE AVERAGE

over 400%   WELL ABOVE AVERAGE

???????????????????

1 Look at the graph of population growth between 1701 and 1981. Compare the different rates of growth in England and Wales, Scotland and Northern Ireland. What reasons can you give for these differences?

2 Describe and account for the changes which took place in the geographical distribution of the population of England and Wales between 1801 and 1881.

Growth of Population

Four things determine whether a country's population increases or decreases – **a** birth rate **b** death rate **c** emigration (people leaving) **d** immigration (people entering). As you can see from the graph on page 65, the population of England and Wales rose steadily from 1701 to 1981, although not always at the same rate. That of Scotland rose slowly, whilst the population of Northern Ireland remained much the same.

The birth rate in England and Wales substantially exceeded the death rate from about 1750 to the early 1930s and again from about 1950 to 1970. At times, both rates rose or fell together, usually because a rise in the birth rate meant a rise in infant mortality. In 1750 a baby only had a 30% chance of living to the age of five years in London. By 1830 the baby's chances of surviving had risen to 70%.

No single reason explains why the birth rate rose or fell, or why the death rate dropped. Epidemics, like those of cholera in the 1830s, help to explain some of the rises in the death rate. The population would have grown even more, but many people emigrated to the United States and the British Empire (as it was up to about 1950).

In the 1950s and 1960s, immigrants from Commonwealth countries made up some of the loss of population due to emigration. But, contrary to popular belief, the number of emigrants has almost always exceeded the number of immigrants.

????????????????????????????

1 Why might reasons for the growth in population between 1740 and 1840 be different from reasons for its growth between 1870 and 1930?

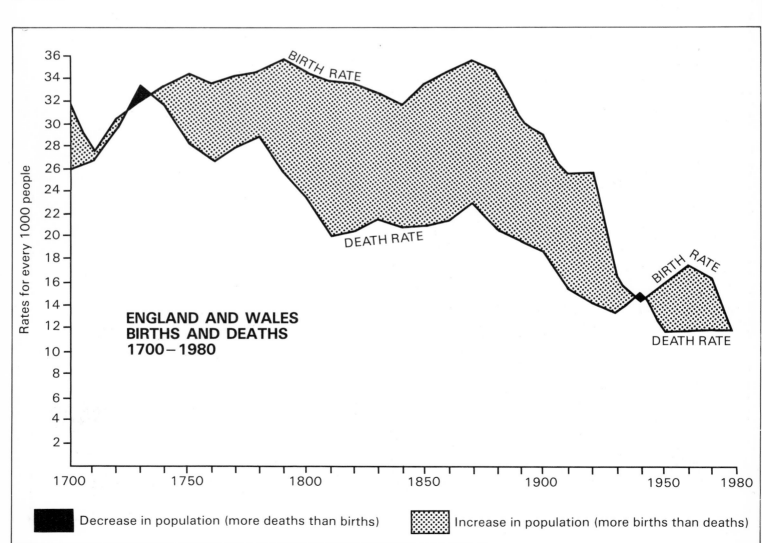

ENGLAND AND WALES BIRTHS AND DEATHS 1700–1980

Rates for every 1000 people

■ Decrease in population (more deaths than births)   ▨ Increase in population (more births than deaths)

REASONS FOR THE DECREASE IN THE DEATH RATE AND RESULTING GROWTH IN POPULATION

DIET
Changes in farming methods meant that Britain produced more wheat, potatoes, meat, milk and dairy products.

In general people had
(1) MORE TO EAT
(2) A HEALTHIER DIET (more proteins and vitamins)

Turnpike roads, canals and later railways enabled food to be taken easily to all parts of Britain; so there were
(3) FEWER FOOD SHORTAGES
(4) NO MAJOR FAMINES (except in Ireland in the 1840s)

ALCOHOLISM
Deaths from alcoholism, due to the widespread availability of cheap gin, were reduced after 1751 when higher taxes made it dear to buy and its sale was controlled.

HYGIENE
Many diseases thrived in town slums where overcrowded, badly ventilated, dirty, damp homes encouraged vermin, flies, coughing and sneezing.
Improvements were badly needed. They included
(1) Cheaper cotton cloth which was easier to keep clean than coarse woollens.
(2) Cheaper soap (from about 1820 onwards).
(3) Cheaper coal—people could keep warm in winter and boil water.
(4) Improved supplies of pure water (from the 1850s).
(5) Better drains and sewers (from the 1850s).
(6) Better housing—poor by modern standards but an improvement on 18th-century slums.
(7) Flush toilets (1900s onwards).
As a result there was a decline in the number of deaths from diseases spread by insects in contact with sewage, manure and decaying rubbish (typhus, infantile diarrhoea), contaminated water and food (typhoid fever, dysentery and cholera) or sneezing and bodily contact in overcrowded homes (tuberculosis, whooping cough, smallpox, measles, scarlet fever and diptheria).

THE PLAGUE
Disappearance of the Plague which killed thousands of people in earlier centuries (e.g. the Black Death in 1348 and the Great Plague of 1665).

BETTER CARE OF INFANTS
(1) Babies were born earlier to healthier mothers.
(2) Fewer orphans were abandoned and left to die (after 1750).
(3) Babies benefitted from all the improvements in diet and cleanliness and warmth.

MEDICAL CARE
(1) New hospitals and improvements in surgery and midwifery in the 18th century.
(2) Use of anaesthetics (1847+) and antiseptics (1867+) in surgery in the 19th century.
(3) Increasing emphasis on the value of fresh air and sea bathing for the well-to-do (from the 1740s onwards).
(4) Greater cleanliness and better nursing in hospitals (1850s onwards).

VACCINATION
Vaccination against smallpox after 1796 saved the lives of many people. In the 18th century smallpox is said to have been responsible for the deaths of over 25% of all infants.

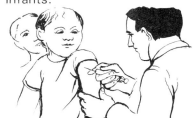

Town Growth and Public Health

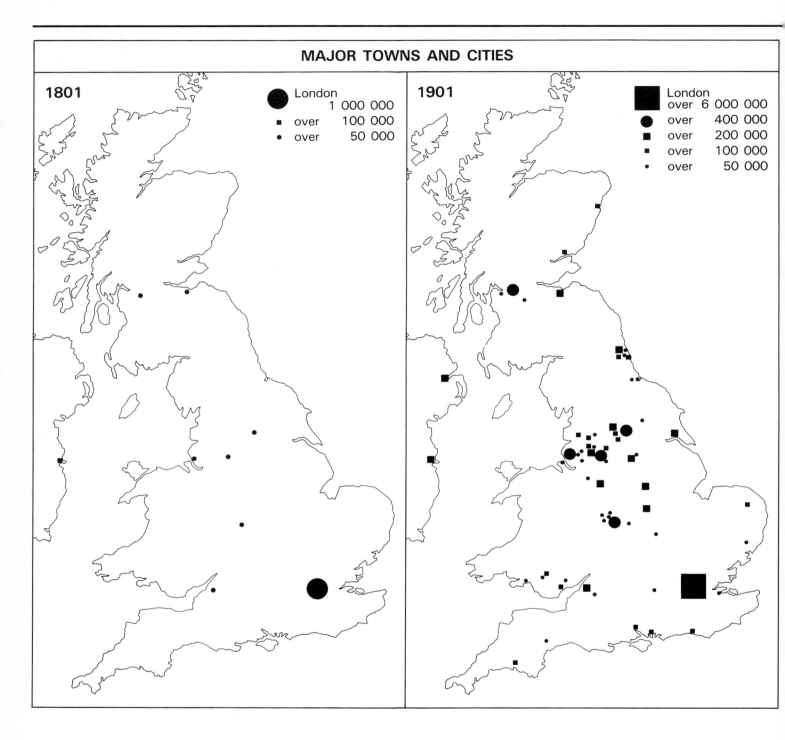

MAJOR TOWNS AND CITIES

1801

London 1 000 000
■ over 100 000
• over 50 000

1901

London over 6 000 000
● over 400 000
■ over 200 000
■ over 100 000
• over 50 000

These maps show the extraordinary growth of towns in the nineteenth century. In fifty years Bradford grew from a small town of 6000 to a large town of 104 000. By 1901 it had a population of 280 000. Cardiff grew from 2000 in 1801 to 164 000 in 1901, and Salford from 14 000 to 221 000 in the same period. In 1801 only eight towns in Great Britain had more than 50 000 people. By 1901 there were over sixty.

??????????????????????????????

1 Describe and account for the growth in the number of large towns between 1801 and 1901.
2 What problems were caused by the rapid growth of the towns? What attempts were made to solve these problems in the nineteenth century?

LIVING CONDITIONS IN THE TOWNS IN THE 1830s

vermin
(Leeds)

nine people sharing
two small rooms
(Stockton)

four people
sharing one bed
(Stockton)

one privy (earth lavatory)
serving several houses
(Birmingham)

stinking cesspools
and overflowing gutters
(most towns)

sixteen homes sharing one water
tap (turned on for only a few
hours each week)
(London)

heaps of dung and
rotting garbage
outside homes
(Liverpool)

sacking instead
of blankets
(Leeds)

no mains sewers
(Manchester)

crowded streets,
alleys and courtyards
—children don't go
to school (Nottingham)

Just a few of the many examples described by travellers in Reports.

TIME LINE: PUBLIC HEALTH IN TOWNS 1830–1875

1831 Cholera epidemic begins in Sunderland and soon spreads.

1832 A total of 53 000 people die from cholera.

1835 Municipal Corporations Act sets up town and borough councils with limited powers (e.g. the supply of gas). Many councils prefer to do nothing since improvements cost money.

1842 Edwin Chadwick publishes his 'Report on the Sanitary Conditions of the Labouring Population of Great Britain'. He shows that the spread of diseases like cholera is due to filth and dirt, damp, overcrowding and lack of pure water; *not* to the fact that people are poor. He recommends better drains, street cleaning and improved water supplies.

1847 Cholera breaks out again and immediately prompts Government action.

1848 The Public Health Act is passed. It establishes a General Board of Health with Chadwick as its chief official. This allows towns to set up Boards of Health with powers to enforce an adequate standard of water supply, drainage and refuse disposal systems. Landowners object to paying rates to finance these improvements and to being forced to improve their properties.

1849 Cholera claims 55 000 victims.

1854 The General Board of Health is disbanded; powerful people say it is unnecessary.

mid 19th century A number of Acts of Parliament are passed giving powers to different types of local authority to clear slums, build homes for working people, control nuisances, etc. But too many of these powers are optional, so many councils and other organisations do nothing rather than raise a rate from local people.

1871 The Local Government Board is established to control local authorities to ensure they carry out Acts of Parliament.

1875 Public Health Act. This gives local authorities new powers to control public health. They have to appoint Medical Officers of Health. They have responsibility for the drains, sewers, water supply and many other matters concerned with public health. They have to ensure that new homes are built with adequate sanitation and water supply. The Artisans Dwellings Improvement Bill gives local authorities the power to pull down slums and erect good houses in their place.

1873 to 1876 Joseph Chamberlain is Mayor of Birmingham and clears a large area of slum dwellings in the city, providing working people's homes in their place. Birmingham Council also takes over the supply of gas and water and purchases the sewage farm.

Medical Advances

In the eighteenth century doctors and surgeons usually killed more patients than they cured. A surgical operation was a very serious matter indeed. There were no anaesthetics to kill the pain of the operation. Instead the patient was given brandy to drink and when intoxicated was held down by burly attendants whilst the surgeon operated as rapidly as possible. Surgeons prided themselves on their speed but this hardly made for accurate, precise surgery. Even if the patient survived the shock of the operation there was a high risk of getting an infection in the operation wound, because the surgeons did not use sterile instruments or wear sterile gowns, gloves and masks; nor did they use antiseptics to kill germs.

LANDMARKS IN THE HISTORY OF MEDICINE

1796 Edward Jenner notices that dairymaids who catch a mild disease called cowpox do not catch smallpox. He successfully vaccinates a boy of 8 by scratching his arm and infecting it with cowpox. The boy fails to catch smallpox when exposed to the disease. Vaccination eventually becomes widespread and saves thousands of lives each year.

1847 Sir James Young Simpson uses chloroform in childbirth. There is opposition at first but this is quelled when Queen Victoria uses it herself in 1853. The use of anaesthetics enables surgeons to take their time during operations without hurting their patients. More complicated operations are possible and fewer patients die from shock.

1854 Florence Nightingale revolutionises nursing in the dirty, overcrowded hospitals filled with wounded from the Crimean War. She insists on cleanliness everywhere and better food. Her work is so successful she devotes the rest of her life to training nurses.

1867 Joseph Lister learns of Pasteur's work on germs and uses carbolic acid to disinfect his operating theatre before and after surgery. He also covers the operation wounds with lint soaked in carbolic acid. Almost immediately the number of his surgical patients to die of septic wounds after an operation drops from 9 out of 20 to 3 out of 20 and eventually to less than 3 out of every 100. This, together with the use of anaesthetics, revolutionises surgery.

1895 Wilhelm Roentgen discovers how to use X-rays which can be used to diagnose ailments inside the body.

1898 Pierre and Marie Curie discover radium and this is later used to treat patients suffering from cancer.

1928 Alexander Fleming first discovers penicillin, a drug which later saves many lives when it is developed during the Second World War.

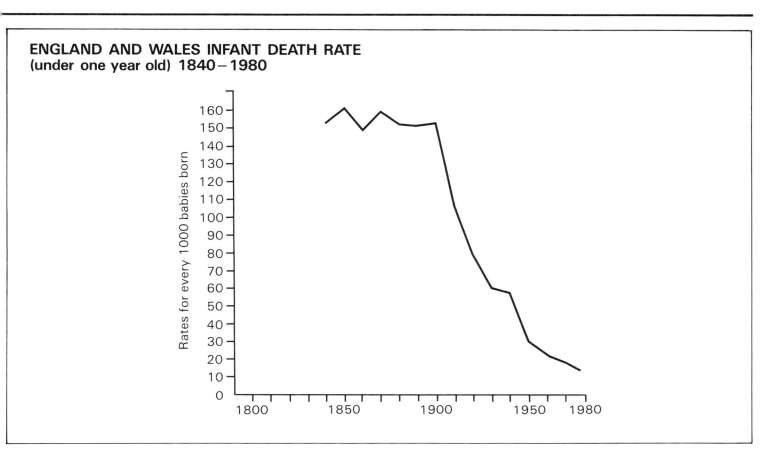

ENGLAND AND WALES INFANT DEATH RATE
(under one year old) 1840–1980

Rates for every 1000 babies born

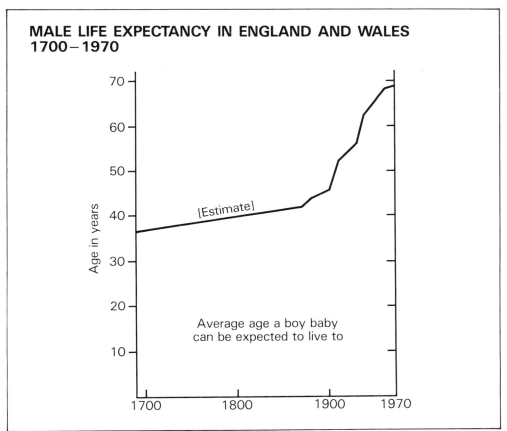

MALE LIFE EXPECTANCY IN ENGLAND AND WALES
1700–1970

Age in years

[Estimate]

Average age a boy baby
can be expected to live to

??????????????????

1   Imagine you are conducting a television interview with a retired doctor in about 1870. Write down what he might have said about the changes in medicine and surgery during his lifetime (between 1795 and 1870).
2   Which do you think was the most important landmark in the history of medicine in the last 200 years?

Education

Opportunities for poor children to go to school were very limited in 1800. Village schools run by a schoolmaster or Dame offered only a rudimentary education at a cost of one or two pennies a week. Poor people had little incentive to send their children to school when they could be sent out to work instead.

In the early nineteenth century Joseph Lancaster and Andrew Bell both developed a new type of school based on the monitorial system. The idea was simple. The teachers taught a group of older boys (*monitors*) and these monitors each taught a smaller group of six to ten pupils. The children were taught to read and write by copying things parrot-fashion (called *rote-learning*).

Out of this monitorial system came the voluntary schools set up by the National Society on Bell's lines. These were run by the Anglican churches. The British and Foreign Society's schools derived from Lancaster's school and were run by Nonconformists. It wasn't until 1833, however, that Parliament first took action and began to pay something towards the cost of educating ordinary people.

SCHOOLS IN THE EARLY NINETEENTH CENTURY

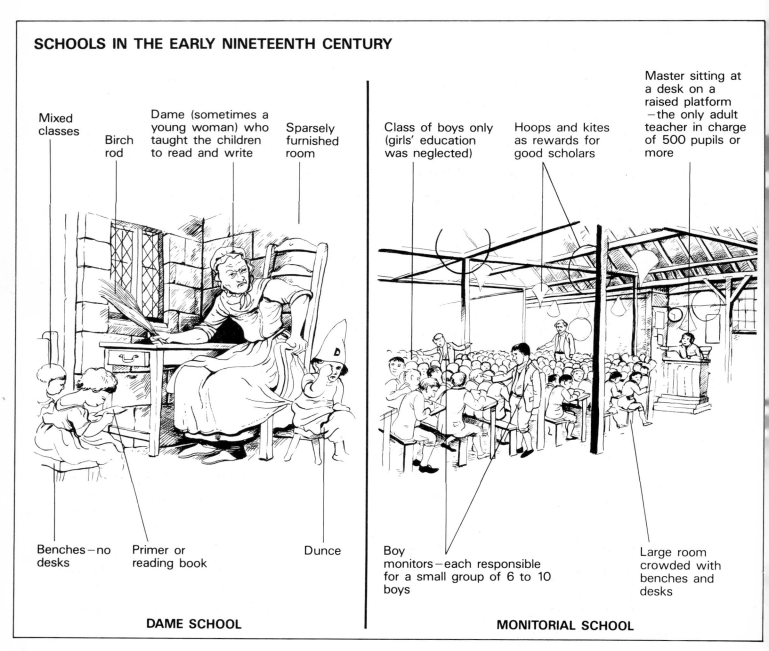

Mixed classes

Birch rod

Dame (sometimes a young woman) who taught the children to read and write

Sparsely furnished room

Benches—no desks

Primer or reading book

Dunce

DAME SCHOOL

Class of boys only (girls' education was neglected)

Hoops and kites as rewards for good scholars

Master sitting at a desk on a raised platform—the only adult teacher in charge of 500 pupils or more

Boy monitors—each responsible for a small group of 6 to 10 boys

Large room crowded with benches and desks

MONITORIAL SCHOOL

TIME LINE: EDUCATION

1833 Parliament grants £20 000 to be used by the voluntary societies to build schools.

1839 The grant is increased to £30 000. Inspectors are appointed to visit schools. Teacher training colleges are founded.

1862 The Revised Code makes payment of the Government grant dependent on children's attendance at school and on their success in a test (conducted by the inspectors) of the three Rs—Reading, Writing and Arithmetic.

1870 W. E. Forster introduces the Education Act
a It divides the country into over 2000 school districts.
b Ratepayers elect people to sit on a school board.
c The school boards are required by law to provide schools *if* no others are available in the district. The money to pay for these new schools is to be raised out of a local rate.
d The school boards are allowed to charge fees and to provide free education for poor children. They can also make attendance at school compulsory for children between 5 and 10 years of age.
e They must provide some religious education but not according to the the teaching of a specific Church. This can still be provided by the voluntary church schools which continue to thrive.

1880 The Mundella Act makes education compulsory for children between 5 and 10.

1891 Education is free for all children under the age of 11.

1899 The school-leaving age is raised to 12.

1902 The Balfour Education Act abolishes the school boards and appoints Local Education Authorities (LEAs) in their place, with the power to provide secondary education for deserving pupils.

1906 Schools are allowed to provide school meals.

1918 The Fisher Education Act raises the school-leaving age to 14.

1926 The Hadow Report recommends that the school-leaving age should be raised to 15 and that 'modern secondary schools' should be built, to provide a more practical education than that of the grammar schools.

1944 R. A. Butler's Education Act raises the school-leaving age to 15 and establishes a system of free secondary education for all pupils. In some areas comprehensive schools are built.

1965 Labour's education minister (Anthony Crosland) compels local education authorities to start planning the reorganisation of their schools on comprehensive lines.

1972 The school-leaving age is raised to 16.

RATIO OF CHILDREN AT SCHOOL TO CHILDREN AT WORK/PLAY 1850–90 (aged 5–10 years)

	AT SCHOOL	AT WORK OR AT PLAY
1850	👤	👤👤👤👤👤👤 👤👤👤👤👤
1860	👤👤👤	👤👤👤👤👤 👤👤👤
1870	👤👤👤👤👤👤	👤👤👤👤👤👤
1880	👤👤👤👤👤 👤👤👤👤👤	👤👤
1890	👤👤👤👤👤👤 👤👤👤👤👤👤	

???????????????????

1 Why did the Government bring in a system of payment by results in 1862? What effects did it have on the schools?

2 Give two reasons why farmers and other employers complained about the 1870 Education Act. Why was this the most important milestone in the history of education in Britain?

The Poor Law

We take it for granted nowadays that adequate provision is made for orphans, the handicapped, the mentally ill, the unemployed and the old. But it hasn't always been so. Most benefits and welfare provisions only date from the present century (see pages 76–79).

In the eighteenth century each parish cared for its poor by

THE POOR LAW BEFORE 1795

Building a *poorhouse* to look after the desperately poor (called *paupers*). They included the old and sick, as well as able-bodied paupers, who were given work to do in return for the *indoor* poor relief they received. This is why it was often called the *workhouse*.

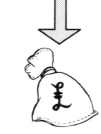

Levying a *Poor Rate* on householders and landowners to pay for the upkeep of the workhouse and to provide *outdoor* poor relief for paupers who didn't live in the workhouse.

Appointing an *overseer* to take charge.

THE SPEENHAMLAND SYSTEM 1795 to 1834

1 In May 1795 the Berkshire magistrates met in the village of Speenhamland intending to fix a minimum wage for farm labourers in the county. There were no trade unions then to negotiate wage rises with the employers. There was much distress at that time because the Napoleonic Wars had led to a rise in food prices.

2 The magistrates decided to urge farmers to raise wages voluntarily. If they were still insufficient, then the labourers' incomes were to be brought up to subsistence level out of the poor rate. Married men with families got more than single people.

3 The Speenhamland System was soon adopted by many other counties. It stopped people starving, but it had many critics because:
a It encouraged labourers to have large families.
b It discouraged farmers from raising wages.
c It didn't reward equal work with equal pay.
d Farm labourers working full-time were treated as if they were paupers living on charity.
e Householders and landowners (who paid rates) were subsidising the wages bill of other employers.
f It caused the poor rate to rise steeply in many parishes.

THE POOR LAW AMENDMENT ACT 1834

In 1834 Parliament passed the Poor Law Amendment Act. This cut the high cost of the poor rate by ensuring that in future only the desperately poor would be driven to seek refuge in a workhouse. The living conditions there were to be appreciably inferior to those of the poorest labourers in work. Poor Law Commissioners were appointed to see that each parish became part of a Union (of parishes) which would elect a Board of Guardians to run the workhouse. They had the power to insist that poor relief be given only to people prepared to live in the workhouse (this was called the *workhouse test*)—with the exception of those 'who shall from Old Age or Infirmity of body be unable to work'.

% OF ALL PEOPLE OVER THE AGE OF 65 WHO WERE PAUPERS

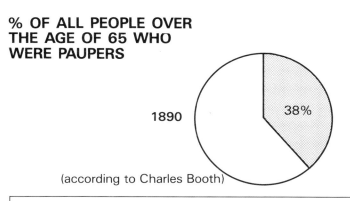

1890   38%

(according to Charles Booth)

?????????????????????????????

1 What were the advantages and disadvantages of the Speenhamland System?
2 What effect did the Poor Law Amendment Act have on the lives of the poor?

At first the 1834 Act was strictly applied and expenditure on poor relief dropped sharply, causing great hardship and distress. But although the system could be made to work in the rural counties it ran into difficulties in the industrial north, where there were several demonstrations. In practice outdoor relief continued to be given to a large number of able-bodied workers, even though they didn't live in the workhouse. Gradually the harshness of the workhouse system softened, but the stigma of being a pauper remained. It deterred many proud, but poverty-stricken, old people from seeking relief. For all its faults the system lasted until 1929 when the powers of the guardians were given to the county and county borough councils.

THE COST OF POOR RELIEF IN ENGLAND AND WALES

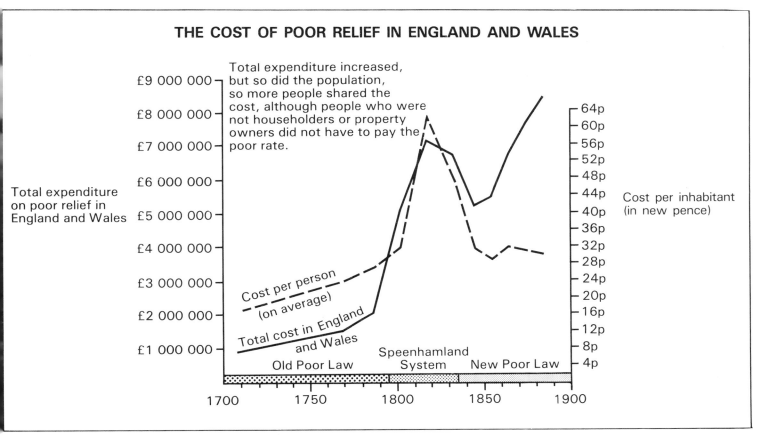

Total expenditure increased, but so did the population, so more people shared the cost, although people who were not householders or property owners did not have to pay the poor rate.

Total expenditure on poor relief in England and Wales

Cost per inhabitant (in new pence)

Cost per person (on average)

Total cost in England and Wales

Old Poor Law   Speenhamland System   New Poor Law

Origins of the Welfare State

The foundations of the Welfare State were laid in the nineteenth century with the Poor Law Amendment Act, the Public Health Acts and other measures. Local authorities were set up to organise social services such as public health, schools and the care of old people.

Government spending on the social services was pitifully small in Victorian times – £27 million in 1890 (the equivalent of about £700 million today) compared with well over £30 000 million in the late 1970s.

Since 1900 the social services have been greatly improved. Two governments in particular were largely responsible for the foundation of the modern Welfare State – the Liberal Government of 1906–1914, and the Labour Government of 1945–1950.

LANDMARKS IN THE DEVELOPMENT OF THE WELFARE STATE (1)

1906 **Workmen's Compensation**—for injuries at work.

1906 **School Meals Act**—meals for poor children.

1907 **The School Health Board**—regular school medical checks.

1908 **The Old Age Pensions Act**—for people over the age of 70 (25p a week from January 1909 onwards). Since it was a *right* and not a form of poor relief, it was welcomed by many old people who had dreaded having to go to the Board of Guardians for help.

1908 **The Children's Charter**—stopped children under 16 buying cigarettes and using public houses. Juvenile courts were established to try children separately from adults. Offenders were sent to Borstals instead of prison.

1909 **The Labour Exchanges Act**—set up labour exchanges all over Britain, to which employers could send details of jobs, and to which the unemployed could go in search of work.

1909 **The People's Budget**—designed by Lloyd George to tax the well-to-do in order to pay for the reforms introduced by the Liberal Government.

1911 **The National Insurance Act**—helped workers earning less than £160 a year to insure against illness. They paid a premium of about 2p a week, which was topped up by the government and the employer. This entitled the insured worker to free medical treatment and sickness benefit. The Act also provided an unemployment scheme for workers in industries where employment was very seasonal. Worker, employer and government each made a contribution. If a workman became unemployed he was entitled to 35p a week for 15 weeks. The Act was introduced by Lloyd George and for a long time people said they 'were on the Lloyd George' if they meant they were receiving unemployment or sick benefit.

1920 **Unemployment Insurance Act**—enlarged the 1911 Act to include most workers earning up to £250 a year. Benefits were increased to 75p a week.

1920 **Housing.** The Coalition Government encouraged local authorities to build council homes out of the rates. Slums were cleared and new estates of houses built.

1925 **Widows, Orphans, Old Age Pensions Act**—provided pensions for the over-65s, widows and orphans.

1929 **Local Government Act**—abolished the Boards of Guardians set up in 1834 by the Poor Law Amendment Act.

1931 The National Government cut unemployment benefit by 10% and introduced the *Means Test* (see page 60).

???????????????????????????

1 Explain how the changes introduced by Liberal governments before 1914 undermined the Poor Law system.
2 Which of the 'causes of poverty' shown in the diagram had been tackled, and with what success, in the years before 1914?

CAUSES OF POVERTY IN 1900

OLD AGE

No pension

UNEMPLOYMENT

No unemployment benefit

SICKNESS

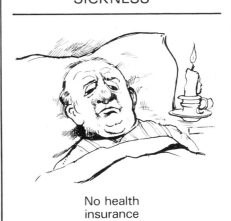

No health insurance

LOW WAGES

No minimum wages in many industries and shops

LARGE FAMILIES

No child benefit; no family income supplement

DISABILITY

No disablement benefit; no compensation for injuries

ONE-PARENT FAMILIES

No widow's benefit; no equal pay

ORPHANS

No orphans' benefit

The Welfare State

The postwar Welfare State envisaged by the Labour Party in 1945 was going to care for everyone 'from the cradle to the grave'. High hopes were entertained for such innovations as the National Health Service and the various services and benefits to be provided by the State. These would ensure an end to poverty and create an educated, healthy and affluent people.

In many respects the Welfare State was a great success, acting as a model for other countries – one of the most comprehensive welfare systems in the world. But unemployment on a massive scale (over three million by 1982), coupled with high rates of inflation (over 20% a year in the early 1980s), put tremendous pressure on the system. Unemployment benefit alone cost billions of pounds, many more people lived long enough to draw a retirement pension, whilst wage increases and price rises made the health, education and other welfare services extremely expensive. By 1977 Government expenditure on the social services was taking 25% of the country's income. Critics wanted to see a reduction in government expenditure on the Welfare State and argued that people drawing state benefits lost their independence and looked to the government for aid, rather than relying on the self-help which was the motto of many Victorians.

LANDMARKS IN THE DEVELOPMENT OF THE WELFARE STATE (2)

1942 Beveridge Report. Sir William Beveridge prepares a report proposing a national health service and a state insurance scheme to improve living conditions and to attack the 'five giants' (see diagram).

1945 The Family Allowances Act provides family benefits.

1945 Housing. Aneurin Bevan tackles the problem of building new homes, and starts by erecting 'prefabs' (prefabricated homes) which are easy to put up.

1946 The New Towns Act plans to build a number of new towns on the outskirts of London (Basildon, Harlow, Crawley, etc.) and other large cities.

1946 The National Health Act is passed (to take effect in 1948). It will provide free medical care for everyone. New hospitals are built and more doctors and nurses trained. But despite this there are still long waiting lists for routine operations.

1946 The National Insurance Act (in operation from 1948 onwards) makes adult insurance compulsory for all workers. It provides unemployment, widow's, maternity and sick benefits among others, as well as the old age pension for men at 65 and women at 60.

1947 Town and Country Planning Act

1948 National Assistance Act provides care and benefit for people in need of assistance, who don't otherwise qualify for benefits under the different State schemes.

1951 National Health Prescription Charges and charges for dental treatment, are introduced (but opposed by Aneurin Bevan and Harold Wilson).

1956 The Clean Air Act is passed to control the amount of smoke over towns. In the early 1950s *smog* (smoke and fog) had killed many people in London.

1961 A Graduated Pensions Scheme is introduced.

1965 The Race Relations Act prohibits racial discrimination.

1970 Equal Pay Act is passed to give women workers the right to equal pay.

1975 Equal Opportunities Act is passed to prohibit discrimination against women.

SIR WILLIAM BEVERIDGE'S FIVE GIANT SOCIAL EVILS (1942)

1 WANT

2 DISEASE

3 SQUALOR

4 IGNORANCE

5 IDLENESS

??????????????????????????????

1 Argue the case either *for* or *against* the Welfare State.
2 Write a dialogue between two of your own elderly relatives discussing the social changes they have seen in their own lifetimes. If possible include anecdotes you have heard them actually use.
3 Which do you think were the three most significant advances in the development of the Welfare State since 1900? What social evils still await effective government action?

Index